THE STATE
**TRETYAKOV
GALLERY**

MASTERPIECES OF THE STATE TRETYAKOV GALLERY

Russian Art from the 12th to early 20th century

PAINTING * DRAWING

SECOND EDITION

RED SQUARE PUBLISHERS

MOSCOW 2007

Published by decision of the Academic Board
of the State Tretyakov Gallery

Director-General Valentin Rodionov

Editor-in-chief Lidia Iovleva

Editors Tatiana Lykova, Irina Volchenkova
Translation Kate Cook
Design and layout Galina Loukachevitch

Masterpieces of the State Tretyakov Gallery. Russian Art from the 12th to early 20th century. Painting. Drawing. Second edition. State Tretyakov Gallery, Moscow, 2007. 160 pp. Illus.
ISBN 978-5-900743-36-3

Among the national art museums of the world the State Tretyakov Gallery holds a special place. Created by the inspired efforts of one man, the dedicated collector Pavel Tretyakov, it evolved from the time of its opening in 1856 into a unique collection of Russian works of art. This invaluable book, richly illustrated with masterpieces of icon painting, pictorial and graphic art from the Gallery's collections, introduces the reader to the main periods in the development of Russian art from the 12th to early 20th century.

ISBN 978-5-900743-36-3

FRONTISPIECE:

Our Lady of Vladimir
First third of the 12th century
Constantinople
Detail

CONTENTS

Our Lady of Vladimir
First third of the 12th century
Constantinople
Tempera on wood
103.8 × 69.1

Mediaeval Russian Art of the 12th to 17th century

Yulia Kozlova

The State Tretyakov Gallery has a first-class collection of mediaeval Russian art, which includes unique mosaics, frescoes, icons, miniatures and works of decorative and applied art. Many of them are historical relics, an integral part of the national spiritual tradition, monuments of folk creativity and a special way of life, which express the moral and aesthetic ideals of the Russian people.

The tradition of painting icons came to Russia from Byzantium together with the adoption of Christianity in 988, and simultaneously Greek terms connected with icon painting appeared in Russian, first and foremost, the word "icon", meaning "image" or "representation". It should be borne in mind that the image here is an unusual one – the visible representation of the invisible, eternal, ideal world, which is inaccessible to the ordinary gaze, yet open to spiritual contemplation.

The adoption of Christianity brought Russia into closer contact with Byzantine culture, yet the selection of elements from the Byzantine ideological and artistic heritage was a creative and independent one and not that of a pupil. The most important thing in Christian culture is the striving for man's inner harmony, his spiritual betterment. This interest in man's spiritual world was expressed most consistently in icon-painting: it is in the icon that the special nature of Russian spirituality with its gentle, contemplative, deep and sincere belief in the creative power of goodness and beauty found embodiment.

From the many specimens of Byzantine painting it was works corresponding to the moral and aesthetic principles of the Russian people that were chosen. In this connection the fate of the Byzantine icon of *Our Lady of Vladimir* which became a highly revered national relic and played a very special role in the history of Russian spirituality is most interesting. The icon was brought to Russia in the first half of the 12th century and placed in a convent at Vyshgorod near Kiev. In 1155 Prince Andrei Bogolyubsky moved it to Vladimir, and in 1158 he founded the majestic Assumption Cathedral for it and gave it a rich icon-case. On 26 August, 1395 during the invasion by Tamerlaine the famous icon was brought to Moscow and on the very same day Tamerlaine retreated, leaving the borders of the Moscow state.

The icon's artistic image is imbued with an austere prayerful mood. The Virgin Mary is caressing her son, pressing him gently to her, with her cheek against his face. The infant has one hand round his mother's neck, while the other is reaching for her face. This iconographical pattern became known as the *Virgin of Tenderness (Eleousa)*. Mary's face is full of sadness and grief. She is looking straight at the viewer, and her expression contains a fleeting premonition of her son's future destiny. The face of the

Infant Christ is serious and concentrated. The faces also stand out for their beautiful pictorial moulding. In the Virgin Mary the warm olive-green tone changes gradually and delicately into pink and red, contrasting with the more gentle and light carnation on the face of the Infant Christ. This masterpiece of world art, which belongs equally to Byzantine and Russian culture, is characterised by an intense spirituality and humanity combined with exceptional pictorial skill. Byzantine icons like *Our Lady of Vladimir* provided Russian masters with models for attaining painterly excellence. By copying and studying them, the masters of mediaeval Russia learnt to create works that were in keeping with national conditions, tastes and ideals. Today the icon of *Our Lady of Vladimir* can be seen in the Church-Museum of St Nicholas the Wonderworker-in-Tolmachi of the Tretyakov Gallery.

One of the oldest icons in the Gallery's collection is the so-called *Ustyug Annunciation* (1130–1140s) which once adorned the St George Cathedral of the Yuriev Monastery in Novgorod and was brought to Moscow in 1561 by Tsar Ivan the Terrible together with other precious Novgorodian relics. Its large dimensions indicate the important role of this image in the interior of the grandiose cathedral, one of the largest in Russia. The structure of the icon is monumental and jubilant. The Virgin Mary is standing, head slightly to one side, listening meekly to the words of the Archangel Gabriel addressed to her: "Hail, thou that art highly favoured, the Lord is with thee" (Luke, 1, 28). The figure of the Virgin, clad in a cerise maphorion (cloak), is calm and majestic. The Archangel, the heavenly messenger, seems lighter and more radiant, full of movement indicated by the refined rhythm of the folds in his robes. The painting of the faces is complex and multi-layered with smooth transitions from shade to lighted areas and modelling devices that go back to the Hellenistic tradition. The connection with the antique heritage can also be seen in the gold lines delineating the archangel's hair. The gold hair, a symbol of greatness and immortality, stresses the luminiferous nature of the image of Gabriel.

In the second half of the 12th century another fine work was produced in Novgorod, the two-sided icon of the *Mandilion* with the *Exaltation of the Cross* on the reverse. The *Mandilion* is thought to have been painted for the Church of the Holy Image on the Sophia side in Novgorod and was later moved to Moscow. Christ's face is surrounded by a halo with a cross and placed on the surface of the icon panel in such a way that the large eyes invested with great expressive power become the compositional centre. The image of Christ impresses one with its austere and majestic beauty. This is emphasised by the gold lines in the hair, a feature that it shares in common with the *Ustyug Annunciation*. The moulding of the face is also similar, soft and fused, with the subtlest transitions from light to shade. The reverse side with the *Exaltation of the Cross* was painted in a different, more temperamental and expressive manner, which calls to mind Novgorodian monumental painting of the late 12th century, in particular, the frescoes at the Church of the Transfiguration of Our Lord at Nereditsa.

Ustyug Annunciation
1130s–1140s
Novgorod
Tempera on wood
238 × 168

Mandilion
Second half
of the 12th century
Novgorod
Tempera on wood
77 × 71

A similar combination of two different painterly manners in one work can be found in another Novgorodian icon of St Nicholas with selected saints in the margins (late 12th – early 13th century), in which there is a perceptible difference between the treatment of the figure of St Nicholas in the central panel and the saints in the margins. This *St Nicholas* comes from the Novodevichy Convent in Moscow, where, legend has it, it was taken from Novgorod by Ivan the Terrible. St Nicholas, bishop of Myra in Lycia (Asia Minor), who lived in the 4th century, was greatly revered in mediaeval Russia for his power to protect from various misfortunes and give assistance in difficult situations. He was known as the "wonderworker", "swift to render help", the "intercessor for peasant folk" and the patron saint of travellers and sailors. In the margins are the saints Cosmas and Damian, Boris and Gleb, Florus and Laurus, Eudoxia, Parasceva and Photinia who were also revered in Novgorod. Nicholas's face with its high forehead, hollow cheeks and tense eyebrows impresses one with its asceticism, spiritual strength, intellect and aristocratic quality. An important role in creating the image is played by the colour range that is determined by the silver background. Silver was a symbol of spiritual purity and chastity. The selected saints in the margins are executed in a different painterly manner and colour range with the use of vermilion, lemon-yellow, bright blue and cerise.

St Nicholas
with Selected Saints
Late 12th –
early 13th century
Novgorod
Tempera on wood
145 × 94

One of the most poetic works of 12th-century Russian icon painting, *Our Lord Emmanuel with Archangels* (late 12th century), comes from Vladimir-Suzdalian Russia. The broad panel contains representations of the head of Christ Emmanuel (with Christ in the form of a youth) and the two archangels. The face of the young Christ is calm and fearless, while those of the two archangels inclined towards him in prayer are contemplative and sad. The sadness is conveyed with a genuinely classical sense of moderation that makes it seem clear, radiant and tranquil. The sense of classical harmony is generated by the leisurely rhythm. The colour combinations are dominated by pale blue and cold pink tones set off by the gentle shimmer of the gold background. An interesting feature is the pink haloes that stress the aristocratic quality of the general colour treatment and help to create an exalted and contemplative mood.

Two fine 13th-century icons of the Virgin Mary are associated with mediaeval Yaroslavl which was founded by Grand Prince Yaroslav the Wise and named after him: the *Virgin Great Panagia (Orans)* and *Our Lady of the Tolga*.

The *Virgin Great Panagia* was most probably painted in the 1220s for the Cathedral of the Transfiguration of Our Lord completed in 1224. The Virgin Mary with a gold medallion bearing Christ Emmanuel on her breast is most majestic. The representation of the Infant Christ surrounded by a gold

← *Our Lord Emmanuel*
with Archangels
Late 12th century
Vladimir-Suzdalian Russia
Tempera on wood
72 × 129

Virgin Great Panagia (Orans)
First third of the 13th century
Yaroslavl
Tempera on wood
193.2 × 120.5

Our Lady of the Tolga
Late 13th century
Yaroslavl
Tempera on wood
140 × 92

halo symbolises Christ's coming to earth and his incarnation by the Virgin Mary. The figure of the Virgin Orans with her arms raised in prayer was perceived as the visual personification and embodiment of the heavenly powers who had taken the city under their protection. The gold, a symbol of the radiance of the Divine light, determines the icon's colouring. The background, the abundant gold highlights and the ornament in combination with purple, the regal colour of the Virgin's cloak, bring out the decorative pearl details on her dress (pearls were a symbol of immaculacy and chastity). The white haloes were probably originally covered with gem-studded gold crowns. The purple, blue, white, red, orange and green are combined by the luminiferous gold into a jubilant, festive chord.

The artistic perfection of the *Virgin Great Panagia* largely determined the subsequent development of Yaroslavl painting. The master who created *Our Lady of the Tolga* at the end of the 13th century was undoubtedly inspired by that well-known splendid work: both icons have several points in common, such as the fibulae (clasps) which symbolise stars on the shoulders and the pearling along the edge of the cloak and on the cuffs. *Our Lady of the Tolga* came from the Tolga Monastery near Yaroslavl founded in 1314. It makes use of an iconography rarely found in Russian icons of the Virgin. Mary is sitting on a throne with the Infant Christ in her lap who is trying to take his first steps. She is holding him with both hands, while he has one arm round

Archangel Michael from the Deisis Tier
Late 14th century – early 15th century
Novgorod
Tempera on wood
86 × 63

her neck and is pressing his cheek to her face. This icon seems gentler and more lyrical thanks primarily to the refined and muted colouring that is subject to the dull glimmer of the silver background. Everything in it creates a mood of concentrated sadness and affection.

The icon of the *Archangel Michael* (late 14th – early 15th century), at one time in the Church of the Resurrection on Lake Myachino in Novgorod, testifies to the diversity of Novgorodian painting at the time of its greatest flowering (the 14th and 15th centuries). The vermilion himation (outer garment), the dominant splash of colour, is draped in broken, angular "Gothic" folds, similar to the sharp lines of the draping on the blue chiton. The vibrant contrast of the vermilion and blue is muted by the silver background. The gold highlights on the wings are quietly melodic. The elegant hands with their long tapered fingers and the asymmetrically painted face add to the impression of delicate beauty in this icon.

The icon of *Paternitas with Selected Saints* (early 15th century), painted at the same time as the *Archangel Michael*, produces a quite different impression. Its composition is full of highly complex theological content. Enthroned in the middle is God the Father. Christ Emmanuel is seated on his lap holding a blue disk with a white dove, a symbol of the Holy Spirit. This is a visual representation of the three persons of the Holy Trinity, God the Father, God the Son and the Holy Spirit. Behind the throne are two six-winged seraphim, and on either

side on pillars the stylites Daniel and Simeon in monk's robes. The white robes of God the Father contrast with the others, in which various shades of brown and ochre dominate: the colour range is in keeping with that of monumental Novgorodian painting in the late 14th century. This icon radiates powerful spiritual energy and the characteristic Novgorodian striving to give convincing visual embodiment to complex theological dogma.

Whereas Novgorodian icon painting at its height impresses with its clear, well thought-out structure, the charm of Pskovian icons lies in their expressive painting, unique colour range, unusually free brushstrokes, and rare iconography. One of the

*Paternitas
with Selected Saints*
Early 15th century
Novgorod
Tempera on wood
113 × 88

Assembly of Our Lady
Late 14th – early
15th century
Pskov
Tempera on wood
81 × 61

finest specimens is the icon of the *Assembly of Our Lady* (late 14th – early 15th century) from the Church of St Barbara in Pskov. The representation on the icon is linked with the text of a stichira sung at Christmastide. According to the words of the stichira, all living things extol the birth of the Saviour and bring him their gifts, thanks and adoration. The whole composition is designed to express joy and jubilation at the birth of Christ and veneration of the Virgin who has given birth to him. Mary is seated against a background of emerald-green hills on a throne with an asymmetrically shaped back, holding an image of Christ Emmanuel surrounded by an eight-pointed glory. The Magi bearing gifts, the singing angels and the awestruck shepherds are advancing towards her. Lower down a reader with an open book and a choir of three deacons are singing the praises of the Saviour and the Virgin. An interesting feature of this icon is the inclusion of two half-naked allegorical figures of the Earth and the Wilderness, which go back to the antique tradition. The figure of the Wilderness is most expressive. She is bringing Christ the gift of a manger and is depicted with considerable foreshortening in rapid motion and bright vermilion drapery. The colouring is based on contrasting dark emerald, orange-red, bright yellow, cerise and white and is most expressive.

The icon of *SS Boris and Gleb on Horseback* belongs to a different artistic tradition, characterised by the striving for a moral ideal and spiritual harmony. Painted in the latter half of the 14th century presumably by an artist who was familiar with the Pskovian tradition, it stood in the Assumption Cathedral of the Moscow Kremlin. The martyr brothers are shown riding on horseback, one turning towards the other as if engaged in a quiet, leisurely conversation. The younger brother, Gleb, depicted as the traditional beardless youth, is gazing at his elder brother with meek devotion. The composition is based on a text that recounts the miraculous appearance of the saints in the form of horsemen to some convicts languishing in prison who had invoked their aid. Boris and Gleb were the first Russian saints and sons of Grand Prince Vladimir of Kiev, who was the brother of Yaroslav the Wise. The brothers were murdered in 1015 by their half-brother Svyatoslav the Accursed and canonised shortly after their death. They were revered as martyrs who accepted death for the sake of Russian unity to overcome enmity and strife and as protectors of the Russian land. They were called the "armour" and "chain-mail" of Russia and likened to a "two-edged sword" against the foe. In this icon their image lacks the heroic element, the accent being placed on spiritual refinement, grace and meekness, particularly in the figure of the younger brother, Gleb.

Our Lady of the Don (1380s–1390s) with the *Dormition* on the reverse belongs to the age of the battle of Kulikovo. It was originally in the Assumption Cathedral in Kolomna, but was moved to the Annunciation Cathedral of the Moscow Kremlin in the reign of Ivan the Terrible. Its iconography is a variation of the Eleousa, which we know from the above description of *Our Lady of Vladimir*. In *Our*

SS Boris and Gleb on Horseback
Second half of the 14th century
Pskov
Tempera on wood. 128 × 67.5

Lady of the Don, however, the hands of Mary and the Infant Christ are arranged differently. Another distinctive feature are Christ's bare legs, which are resting on the Virgin's left wrist. The emotions expressed here are also different. *Our Lady of the Don* impresses one by its meditative quality, its gentle, quiet sadness. The silhouette of the Virgin's head has a refined beauty. Her face radiates love and goodness and is painted in a soft fused manner. The deep blue details shine like precious stones: the band on Christ's shoulder, the tiny scroll in his hand, and the head drape and sleeve of the Virgin's chiton. The intensity of the blue is enhanced by the gold on the Infant's robes and the edge of the Virgin maphorion. The *Dormition* on the reverse is treated in a different, more expressive manner, reminiscent of monumental fresco painting. Many specialists believe that the two sides were painted by different artists – *Our Lady of the Don* by Theophanes the Greek (circa 1340 – circa 1410) and the *Dormition* by another master from the famous icon-painter's workshop.

The icon of the *Annunciation* which came from the Trinity-St Sergius Lavra also belongs to the end of the 14th century. It is interesting to compare it with the 12th-century image of the *Ustyug Annunciation* described above. In the older icon everything has a solemn static quality, whereas the 14th-century composition contains complex, highly dynamic space formed by the bizarre architecture. The movement running through the architecture echoes the action which is taking place in the scene: the swiftly

← Theophanes the Greek (?)

Our Lady of the Don
1380s–1390s
Moscow
Tempera on wood. 86 × 67

striding archangel is addressing the Virgin Mary who bows meekly in response to his words. The curving lines of the Virgin's silhouette are repeated in the architectural forms subject to rhythms that anticipate the harmonic structures in Andrei Rublev's works.

The work of Andrei Rublev (circa 1370 – circa 1429) is traditionally regarded as the height of Russian icon-painting. His art embodies the ideal of spiritual meditation, emotional harmony and moral perfection elaborated by the Venerable Sergius of Radonezh, the founder and first father superior of the Trinity-St Sergius Monastery.

His *Saviour* and *Archangel Michael* (early 15th century) formed part of the Deisis tier from Zvenigorod. The spiritual power of the icons of the Zvenigorod tier inspired worshippers to strive for moral perfection and the attainment of spiritual harmony. The Saviour's face is full of quiet compassion and radiates goodness and love. In his features one can sense the Russian ideal of beauty: the small eyes, high cheekbones, slender neck and golden tinge of the pale brown hair and beard. At the same time this feeling of active love and compassion is combined in the image of Rublev's *Saviour* with a kind of aloofness, almost inaccessibility for the viewer. The *Archangel Michael* does not seem so remote, because his face is painted closer up than that of the Saviour. The painting of the *Archangel* is a radiant constellation of pure blue, pink, golden and ochre tones.

Annunciation
Late 14th century
Constantinople (?)
Tempera on wood. 43 × 34

Andrei Rublev's greatest work and the peak of his art was his *Trinity* (1425–1427), the most beautiful and perfect Russian icon. It was painted for the iconostasis of the Trinity Cathedral in the Trinity-St Sergius Monastery. It shows the triune Godhead in the form of three angels seated around a table, in the middle of which is a cup, the symbol of Christ's redeeming sacrifice. The icon can be interpreted in different ways. According to one version, the angel

Andrei Rublev   →

Old Testament Trinity. 1425–1427
Moscow
Tempera on wood. 142 × 114

in the middle stands for the second person in the Trinity, Christ, because it is attired in his traditional robes, a cerise chiton with a gold band on the shoulder and a blue himation. The angel on Christ's right is the first person of the Trinity, God the Father, and the one on his left the Holy Spirit. Each detail of the composition is full of deep meaning: the chambers behind God the Father symbolise the wisdom of the divine ordering of the universe and also the earthly church; the tree in the middle bending over Christ is the tree of life and the rock behind the Holy Spirit, a symbol of the sublime and also a sign of spiritual stamina and strength. The composition itself, based on simple geometrical structures, is also full of complex significance: the three angels enclosed in a triangle symbolise the triune godhead, the triangle enclosed in an octagon is a symbol of eternity and the whole enclosed in a circle, a sign of supreme and eternal harmony. Smooth circular rhythms unite all the details into a single harmonious image. The beauty and purity of the colour and the perfection and majestic simplicity of the composition convey clearly and visually the most important dogma of Orthodoxy, the equality and oneness of the three hypostases of the Godhead. As well as its complex theological significance the icon had a perfectly real and relevant meaning for Andrei Rublev's contemporaries, which was associated with concrete events in Russian life at that time. Legend has it that the *Trinity* was painted in honour of the Venerable Sergius of Radonezh, who established the cult of the three-in-one Godhead in Russia – "and

gazing upon the Holy Trinity we do overcome fear of the hateful strife of this world" for the triumph of the ideal of the harmony and unity of Russian people. Andrei Rublev's *Trinity* is rightly considered one of the most perfect expressions of the Russian people's aesthetic and moral ideals.

Whereas a poetic, meditative trend dominated painting in Central Russia throughout the 14th and 15th centuries, the art of Novgorod developed in a different key, marked by more expression and inner energy and sometimes inspired by the ideals of Novgorodian independence and resistance to the unifying policy of the Moscow state. A striking example of this is the icon of the *Battle of the Novgorodians with the Suzdalians* (mid-15th century), sometimes referred to in the literature as the "Sign from the icon of Our Lady". The subject is based on a real historical event. In February 1170 the combined armies of several Russian principalities led by Mstislav Andreyevich, Andrei Bogolyubsky's son, marched on Novgorod and laid siege to it. On 25 February a battle took place that ended in the total and devastating defeat of the men of Suzdal. The miraculous liberation of Novgorod from the enemy who were vastly superior in numbers is reflected in chronicles and oral tradition. According to Novgorodian legends, the town was saved by the miraculous intercession of the wonder-working icon of *Our Lady of the Sign*, which has survived to this day and is now in the St Sophia Cathedral in Novgorod.

The painter of the icon appears to have a good knowledge of the various legends and depicts the

Andrei Rublev

Deisis (Zvenigorod tier)
Early 15th century
Moscow
Tempera on wood

Archangel Michael
158 × 108

Saviour   →
158 × 106
Detail

*The Miracle of Our Lady
of the Sign (Battle of the
Novgorodians with the
Suzdalians)*
Late 15th century
Novgorod
Tempera on wood
133 × 90

Our Lady of Tenderness (Lyubyatovo)
Mid-15th century
Pskov
Tempera on wood. 109 × 77

event in the form of three consecutive and inter-connected episodes. The composition is divided into three registers, one for each episode. The upper register, the largest, shows the carrying of the won-der-working icon from the Church of the Saviour in Ilyina Street to the St Sophia Cathedral on the opposite bank of the Volkhov. The middle section shows the icon placed on the city wall, behind which the people of Novgorod are hiding. From the city gates the elders have gone out to parley with the Suzdalians, who break their promise and start firing arrows at the walls and the icon of Our Lady. The lower register depicts the victory of the men of Novgorod: their army is riding out of the gateway of a fortified tower, led by three warrior saints, SS George, Boris and Gleb, who are helping to rout the Suzdalians. The latter are faltering, their banners collapsing – a symbol of defeat. Created in the mid-dle of the 15th century, this icon reminded Novgorodians of their glorious past victories and the protection of the miraculous icon and foretold future battles with Central Russia, for at that time the Suzdalians were associated with the Muscovites. It is a clear reflection of the diplomatic and political tension between Novgorod and Moscow on the eve of the annexation of Novgorod to the Moscow state.

An aura of poetic legend surrounds the mid-15th century icon of *Our Lady of Tenderness (Lyubya-tovo)* formerly in the St Nicholas Monastery at Lyubyatovo near Pskov. Legend has it that in 1570 on his way to Pskov "to slay the Pskovians" Tsar Ivan the Terrible spent the night in the monastery. As he stood in church the next morning listening to the singing and gazing at the wonder-working icon of *Our Lady of Tenderness* the Tsar had a change of heart and said to his men "let the killings cease". In 1581 when the army of King Stefan Bathory of Poland laid siege to Pskov, his soldiers axed the icon: traces of their blows can still be seen on the painting and there is a hole in the panel by the right margin. In spite of the damage the painting has survived fair-ly well and the sad, gentle expression on the Virgin's

*The Dormition
of the Virgin*
Late 15th century
Tver
Tempera on wood
113 × 88

face is quite delightful, as well as the intimate gesture of the Infant touching Mary's cheek. Note the
Pskovians' favourite colours with vermilion pre-
dominant, and a rare detail, the vermilion haloes
with a gold foliate pattern.

For almost two centuries Tver competed with
Moscow for the role of national Russian ideological
and political centre. Tver had its own artistic tradition and original local icon painting. One of the
finest specimens of the Tverian school is the
Dormition (second half of 15th century) nicknamed
the "Blue" because of its unusual colouring in which
various shades of blue dominate. The composition
is based on apocryphal texts and teachings of the
Holy Fathers relating to the passing away of the
Virgin Mary. This particular iconographical pattern
was known as the *Cloud Dormition* because it
includes the figures of apostles floating on clouds
and accompanied by angels. It is said that the apostles were miraculously transported to the Virgin's
house from all corners of the earth and were present
at her passing away. Christ descended from heaven
to receive the Virgin's soul in the form of the swad-
dled infant that Christ is holding. In the upper part
of the composition, in the centre, we see the ascension of the Virgin with a rather rare episode, the pre-
senting of her girdle to the Apostle Thomas. An
account of the Dormition says that the Apostle
Thomas arrived late when the Virgin was already
ascending into Heaven, and received her girdle in
remembrance of her. Among the apostles standing
by Mary's couch are several grieving women of

Jerusalem and two prelates. The complex multi-figured composition, which includes several episodes
that took place at different times and places, shows
a classical clarity of structure, a beautiful rhythmic
pattern and aristocratic colouring.

In the second half of the 15th century the art of
Moscow was stylistically diverse, but the tendency
to create an image of heavenly bliss, an ideal world
based on love and harmony, remained prevalent. It
was embodied most fully in the work of Dionysius
(circa mid-15th – early 16th century). Like Rublev he
combined the talent of a monumentalist with the gift
of icon painting. In 1482 in the Ascension Convent
of the Moscow Kremlin an icon of the Virgin
Hodegetria was damaged by fire. It was "of Greek
painting" and, as the chronicle says, "Dionysius the
icon-painter did paint another on the same panel in
the same image". In Dionysius's *Virgin Hodegetria*
(1482) the stateliness and majesty of the silhouette
are combined with the enamel-like smoothness and
virtuoso modelling typical of this master in the painting of the faces.

In 1500 Dionysius painted icons for the Trinity
Cathedral of the Pavel Obnorsk Monastery near
Vologda, which is where this *Crucifixion* comes
from, adding to our knowledge of the character of
the master's work. In the middle is the cross with the
crucified body of Christ, to the right of the cross is
the Virgin with the women of Jerusalem and to the
left Christ's favourite disciple John the Divine and
Longinus the Centurion. An interesting feature are
the angels weeping over the cross and figures, rarely

← Dionysius

Virgin Hodegetria. 1482
Moscow
Tempera on wood. 135 × 111

found in the Russian tradition, of the defeated Old Testament church flying away and the New Testament church coming to take its place. The icon has no dramatic or tragic resonance and is full of noble contemplation, aloofness and luminescence. The colours are bright and clear, and the cold tones glitter like gems on the gold background.

The work of Dionysius was to influence 16th-century Russian painting for a long time to come, but in the age of Ivan the Terrible new traditions gradually developed that were characterised, on the one hand, by a kind of didactic academism and urge to conserve established compositional and pictorial devices and, on the other, a desire for elegance and refined beauty.

The icon of *St Demetrius of Salonica* (circa 1583) painted for the Church of St Demetrius in the Nikitsky Monastery in Moscow belongs to the final years of Ivan the Terrible's reign. The church was renovated in connection with the birth of the tsar's son Dmitri in 1582. The martyr warrior and patron saint of Tsarevich Dmitri is shown in armour with a spear and shield in his hand and a helmet that reminds one of West European Renaissance helmets, but also with a crown, the symbol of martyrdom, on his head. In his figure the accent is placed not on the heroic aspect, but on his aristocratic elegance, refinement and courtly grace. An important role is played by ornamental motifs, which echo the patterns on the splendid jewellery of Ivan's day. The olive tones, dense green and dark ochre of the face add a somewhat sombre touch.

Dionysius

Crucifixion. 1500
Moscow
Tempera on wood
85 × 52

St Demetrius of Salonica
16th century (circa 1583 ?)
Moscow
Tempera on wood
119 × 86.5

Prokopy Chirin

St Nicetas the Warrior. 1593
Stroganov school
Tempera on wood
29 × 22

The tendency towards refinement characteristic of this age was developed and continued in the art of the so-called Stroganov school, artists who had matured in the service of the royal court, but who carried out unofficial commissions for, inter alia, the Stroganovs, wealthy industrialists in the Russian North. The icon of *St Nicetas the Warrior* painted in 1593 by Prokopy Chirin (?– circa mid-17th century) helps us to get an idea of this school. Nicetas the martyr is depicted in a prayerful pose. His figure is delicate and barely touches the ground. Bright as enamel or precious stones the colours shine on the dark olive background typical of many Stroganov icons. An interesting feature is the icon's small size and the consequent miniature manner of painting in which purely graphic devices found in engraving and jewellery prevail.

The second half of the 17th century was an extremely rich and interesting time, when the long traditions of mediaeval Russian culture were on the way out and the art of the new age was emerging. Simon Ushakov (1625–1686) was the leading master of this period. The icon of *The Tree of the State of Muscovy (The Exaltation of Our Lady of Vladimir)* was painted by Ushakov for the Trinity Church-in-Nikitniki in Moscow in 1668, as can be read on the reverse. In the centre is a medallion with *Our Lady of Vladimir*, the famous icon and palladium of Moscow. The wonder-working icon is surrounded by the branches of a symbolical tree growing out of the Assumption Cathedral in the Kremlin. At the roots of the tree are the founders of the Moscow state, Metropolitan Peter and Prince Ivan Kalita. On the branches are medallions showing tsars, hierarchs, prelates and fools-in-Christ, including Alexander Nevsky, Ivan the Terrible's sons Theodore and Dmitri, Sergius of Radonezh, Basil the Blessed and other saints, who by their feats and piety enhanced the authority of Moscow as the national spiritual and political centre. The composition also includes portraits of the tsar reigning at that time, Alexis, with his first wife Maria and their two sons, Alexis and Theodore. Thus real and symbolical space are united, as it were, but on the whole the structure of the icon is traditional and convention-

Simon Ushakov

Our Lady of Eleousa (Kikkotissa). 1668
Armoury. Moscow
Tempera on wood. 130 × 76

al. This combination of a traditional scheme with details taken from real life, West European engravings or book illustrations, is typical of many icons of this period. In the same year, 1668, Simon Ushakov painted the icon of *Our Lady of Eleousa (Kikkotissa)* which was a copy of the very early wonder-working icon of *Our Lady of Eleousa*, a sacred relic of the island of Cyprus. This explains why the icon bears the words "Eleousa Kikkotissa" in Greek and a Greek inscription on the scroll.

The new secular forms and views of art that were gradually taking shape within mediaeval Russian icon-painting finally emerged in the period of Peter the Great's reforms. Yet even after these reforms the centuries-long heritage of mediaeval Russian art continued to influence national artistic culture and was preserved in icon painting, in which traditional forms coexisted with works close to secular portraiture or genre painting.

Simon Ushakov

The Tree of the State of Muscovy
(The Exaltation of Our Lady of
Vladimir). 1668
Armoury. Moscow
Tempera on wood
105 × 62

Unknown artist (first quarter
of the 18th century)

*Portrait of Anastasia
Naryshkina with
her children Alexandra
and Tatiana*
Oil on canvas. 180.2 × 130.8

Painting. 18th to the first half of the 19th century

SVETLANA STEPANOVA

The art of the eighteenth and the first half of the nineteenth century in fact covers two historical periods. The unique character of this time span was determined by the specific *historical and cultural situation in Russia, which up to the eighteenth century had developed outside European culture of the modern age. The mediaeval artistic tradition embodied the idea of the world and man in the sacral form of church art, which had no division into genres. Secular subjects did not appear until the second half of the seventeenth century in the form of the so-called* parsuna *and* parsuna *portrait, which combined canonical iconographical devices and conventional representation with scrupulous accuracy in conveying the person's appearance and details of the dress. The range of sitters was practically limited to royal monarchs. The historic reforms of Russian state and political life aimed at making the country more European led to fundamental changes in the cultural sphere and everyday life.*

In little more than a century a secular culture was established which produced new forms of representational art and a new artistic language

While retaining its link with the traditions of the preceding age, the art of the first half of the nineteenth century acquired a special character. The new historical conditions and evolution of style found expression in the artistic phenomenon of romanticism, which in turn nurtured the seeds of realism. The specific feature of Russian art of the eighteenth and first half of the nineteenth century is the coexistence of different stylistic trends, which did not affect the unity of artistic culture during this time.

The formation of a European type of Russian aristocracy is recorded most visually in portraiture.

The lack of a national tradition made it necessary to study. Without a proper mastery of the devices of the West European school it would have been impossible to develop the artistic genres for what Peter's reforms required of them. It was not only aristocratic tastes that changed rapidly. The level of demand for art works also increased dramatically. And the borrowing of ready-made models facilitated the work of the artist, freeing him from possible compositional and pictorial difficulties.

The broad cultural contacts that were established in the reign of Peter the Great underwent various changes connected with the development of Russian social life. Without relinquishing state prestige or national dignity, such monarchs as Peter the Great

Ivan Nikitch Nikitin   →
Portrait of Count Gavriil Golovkin. 1720s
Oil on canvas. 90.9 × 73.4

and Catherine the Great sought to adapt to Russian requirements that which was fruitful in European art. They invited foreign masters, sent Russian artists abroad and acquired art collections, all of which promoted the rapid development of Russian culture. The work of foreign masters in Russia constitutes a special phenomenon in Russian culture known as *rossika*. The canvases of Louis Caravaque, Johann Heinrich Wedekind and Georg Christoph Grooth in the Gallery display add to our idea of the development of secular art and the stylistic features of the period. The works produced by L. Tocque, Jean-Louis Voille, Pietro Rotari, Stefano Torelli and Johann Baptist Lampi form an integral part of the general picture of eighteenth-century artistic life in the interaction of all its components.

Petrine period portraiture is represented in the Gallery collection by a few precious paintings ranging widely from the "Preobrazhensky Series"of Peter's rowdy youthful companions with their sharp, somewhat coarse characterisation to the works of I.N. Nikitin.

The portrait of Anastasia Yakovlevna Naryshkina with her children Alexandra and Tatiana by an unknown artist of the first quarter of the 18th century is a characteristic example of early secular painting. In spite of the technical flaws in the drawing and composition, this is one of the most interesting works of the 18th century in the Gallery's collection. The family painting of the lady with her two daughters is executed in the style of an official portrait intended to produce a certain impression on the viewer. The close-up, frontal composition, the striking costumes and colour treatment create a most memorable image. The sombre background with a barely visible monumental column enhances the effect of the three figures that form a vivid decorative group. The lady is wearing a somewhat bizarre bonnet, the little girls are dressed in adult clothes with wigs on their heads, and all three are posing self-consciously for the artist. But behind the outer artificiality of the gestures, poses and fashionable clothes, one can sense the true originality of these Russian figures and the lively spirit of the age.

The age of Petrine reforms combined both interest in the individual with his clearly expressed social status, the observance of European cultural standards with traditional customs and beliefs that were hard to discard. This fusion of Europeanism and national tradition, the urge for change and the power of conservative popular instincts, gave the culture of the Petrine period a special freshness and acerbity. The lady in the portrait was Princess Myshetskaya before her marriage to K.A. Naryshkin, a typical member of Peter's group of reformers and public figures. The last royal carver (*kravchy*), a court post under Tsar Alexis, he became chief commandant at Dorpat, first commandant of St Petersburg and later governor of Moscow.

The name of Ivan Nikitich Nikitin (circa 1680–1742) is associated with the first significant advances of Russian portraiture. Exceptionally talented, he was a favourite of Peter the Great and became the first artist sent abroad to study by the emperor. After

Ivan Vishnyakov

Portrait of Prince Fyodor Golitsyn as a Child. 1760
Oil on canvas. 119.3 × 68.2

Alexei Antropov

Portrait of Anastasia Izmailova. 1759
Oil on canvas. 57.2 × 44.8

visits in 1716–1719 to Venice and Florence, where he studied at the Florentine Academy, Nikitin returned to St Petersburg and became court painter. His early works, which were executed before his study visit to Italy and testify to his unusual talent, include portraits of members of the royal family, Tsarevna Natalia Alexeyevna, Peter's sister (not later than 1716) and Peter's eldest daughter Anna (not later than 1716). They combine a keen feeling for nature with an original understanding of baroque painterly devices.

His portrait of Count Gavriil Ivanovich Golovkin (1720s), a supporter of Peter the Great, who was state chancellor and president of the Collegium of Foreign Affairs is a real masterpiece. Having completely mastered the pictorial technique and stylistics of the West European portrait tradition, Nikitin creates here an image of an energetic, intelligent and efficient individual in the age of reform.

The work of Ivan Yakovlevich Vishnyakov (1699–1761) shows a kind of return to *parsuna* painting with its fixed and simplified system reduced to a most laconic, yet effective type of compositional and colour treatment. The artist makes the individual characterisation of the figures and the painterly technique more complex, however, attaining a rocaille elegance in the details and a refinement of colouristic nuances. Vishnyakov led the "painting team" at the Chancellery of Buildings, which carried out various sorts of artistic work and also served as an art school at that time. In his portrait of Prince Fyodor Nikolayevich Golitsyn as a child (1760) Vishnyakov creates a typical 18th-century image of the "adult child", whose destiny is determined by his social origin and family status. The boy's gentle face is illumined with a serious, intent expression, his pose is sedately static, and all the accessories on the uniform of the Horse Guards, for which his name has already been put down, are reproduced with great care. The combination of velvety black and bright red on the uniform and the gold embroidery give it a special festive air.

The official portrait was the most widespread type in the eighteenth century and its main purpose was to demonstrate the sitter's social standing. The small-sized portrait that gradually became widespread in the middle of the century was often a condensed version of a larger formal portrait and retained all its official qualities. This important stage in the development of the private portrait is associated with the work of Alexei Petrovich Antropov (1716–1795). Like other Russian artists of his day, he engaged in all manner of artistic activities and had his own painting school. His pupils included D.G. Levitsky and P.S. Drozhdin. The vivid characters of his sitters, his desire to record all their distinctive features and his love of rich, local colour give his canvases a special touch of clear, profound simplicity and true originality. His portrait of lady-in-waiting Anastasia Mikhailovna Izmailova (1759) is one of the artist's finest works, thanks to the expressive image of the sitter and the beauty of the painting. The lady-in-waiting of Empress Elizabeth, she appears in this portrait as a strong, outstanding personality. Her image embodies the most striking aspects of the active and masterful female temperament and is a kind of symbol of the age.

An exceptional role in the development of the Russian school of painting belongs to the Imperial Academy of Arts founded in 1757. Thanks to the direct assistance of I.I. Shuvalov and I.I. Betsky, its founding and development were based on the principles of the great European schools, first and foremost, the French Royal Academy of Painting. In the curriculum priority was given to drawing and composition, but the history genre, which at that time was not yet firmly established in Russian painting was regarded as the most important. The first and major history painter of the eighteenth century was Anton Pavlovich Losenko (1737–1773). After receiving an excellent training in Paris (where he was awarded silver medals) and also in Rome, the artist embodied in his work the classical artistic ideals of the Age of Enlightenment. The inner content of his painting *Hector Taking Leave of Andromache* (1771) based on Homer's "Iliad" (book 6) is the clash of civic duty and personal emotion, typical of classical

Anton Losenko

Hector Taking Leave of Andromache. 1773
Oil on canvas. 155.8 × 211.5

ethics. The expressiveness and tragedy of the scene, which unfolds before the viewer as if on the stage, is conveyed in the composition and dynamics of the group and the rhetorical gestures and poses of each figure. The hot colouring of reddish and brown tones and the energetic brushwork, which records the masses and foreshortening with bold precision and conveys the movement of the figures in space, testify to the artist's exceptional talent and mastery.

Genre paintings came low down in the academic hierarchy and existed, as a rule, in pastoral, allegorical or folkloric form. The canvases *A Peasant Dinner* (1774) and *Celebrating a Marriage Contract* (1777) by Mikhail Shibanov are an unusual phenomenon in the art of this period. Of peasant stock, Mikhail Shibanov (? – not before 1789) came to St Petersburg thanks to Admiral G.A. Spiridov as a master skilled in various artistic trades. Here he received a thorough professional training outside the Academy of Arts and worked later for G.A. Potemkin. His genre paintings have an epic quality both in scale of representation and in the ritual solemnity of

the action that is taking place. In this respect they are close to the iconographic monumental tradition, but executed with the devices of history painting. The artist also seeks to record for the viewer the characteristic features of local life. Both paintings show peasants from the Suzdal area. Shibanov depicts the customs, headwear, and embroidery motifs widespread in these parts with great accuracy. Thus, for the first time in Russian art the ethical and spiritual foundations of popular life were embodied in genuine realistic, large-scale artistic form.

Mikhail Shibanov

Celebrating a Marriage Contract. 1777
Oil on canvas. 199 × 244

Detail   →

← Ivan Argunov

Portrait of an Unknown Woman
in Russian Costume. 1784
Oil on canvas. 67 × 53.6

The peasant theme receives different treatment in I.P. Argunov's *Portrait of an Unknown Woman in Russian Costume* (1784). The majestic serenity of this handsome woman, the beautifully conveyed folk costume characteristic of a wet nurse in the Moscow gubernia, the refined drawing and smooth painting create an impression of spiritual purity and artistic perfection. A serf of the Sheremetev counts, Ivan Petrovich Argunov (1729–1802) did not receive a systematic education, but was nevertheless one of the leading artists of his day, whose pupils included Anton Losenko.

In the second half of the eighteenth century the portrait genre reached such a high level of artistic culture that it could solve various challenging tasks. In the work of the leading portraitists of this period, F.S. Rokotov, D.G. Levitsky and V.L. Borovikovsky, one can observe the final moulding of artistic and image devices into a unified artistic world view and aesthetic canon. The idea of the ideal citizen was linked with the harmonic combination of the public and the private expressed in the moral and intellectual standing of the gentry. Now that their work was no longer organised in workshops with their restrictive corporate rules and norms, the type of artist also changed.

Fyodor Stepanovich Rokotov (1735?–1808), who was admitted to the Academy of Arts "at the verbal insistence" of I.I. Shuvalov, was one of the first Russian artists to be granted the title of academician of painting. In the Rokotov type of portrait we find the completion of the process by which artistic form became more complex in keeping with the growing demand and the refined taste of the enlightened gentry. The highest achievement in the sphere of the official portrait was the coronation portrait of Catherine the Great (1763), the sketch for which was made in Moscow. The expressiveness of the composition which is based on a profile turn of a seated figure, rarely found in official portraits, the plastic precision of the Empress's commanding gesture, and the careful selection of accessories serve to enhance the idea of the noble monarch's royal greatness. Catherine's regal presence and the rich colour of the scumbled painting create a highly memorable artistic image.

Rokotov won most recognition as a master of the private portrait who created the illusion of subtle emotional states, elusive volatility and rare spirituality in his models. They show a kind of "family" resemblance, yet, at the same time, they are uniquely individual: the elegance of the slightly haughty E.N. Orlova (circa 1779) is far removed from the touching, tremulous air of A.P. Struiskaya (1772), just as the clever "omniscience" of V.E. Novosiltseva (1780) is quite unlike the restrained reserve of A.Yu. Kvashnina-Samarina (first half of 1770s). The compositional and painterly devices are often repeated. In his private portraits Rokotov reduces to a minimum the signs of social status which were obligatory for an artist. In Russian painting, however, there was no great difference between official and private portraiture. A person's private life was seen as one of the forms of his public life, bearing the stamp of the

Fyodor Rokotov
Portrait of Vasily Maikov. 1775
Oil on canvas. 60 × 47.8

Fyodor Rokotov   →
Portrait of Catherine the Great. 1763
Oil on canvas. 155.5 × 139

standards of behaviour and manner accepted by the gentry. Vasily Ivanovich Maikov (1775) gazes at the viewer with a faintly ironical smile on his politely benign face. A retired guards captain, poet and man of letters of the M.M. Kheraskov circle, he appears in Rokotov's portrait as the embodiment of the ideal gentleman of Catherine the Great's age, whose education and intellect give him a sense of dignity and inner freedom.

Dmitri Grigorievich Levitsky (1735–1822) was a master of great creative power. His painterly manner was flexible and diverse. He trained under his engraver father, then with A.P. Antropov, and possibly took lessons from Louis Jean François Lagrene, J. Valeriani and G.I. Kozlov. Levitsky's skill, inventiveness and free handling of the established portrait canon produced the richness of plastic ideas and portrait characteristics that place him at the very top

← Dmitri Levitsky

Portrait of Prokopy Demidov. 1773
Oil on canvas. 222.6 × 166

of the achievements of eighteenth-century Russian portraiture. While observing the scheme of official representation in his portrait of Prokopy Akinfievich Demidov (1773), the artist complicates the characterisation by adding the sitter's purely personal qualities, the condescending self-irony of a man who knows his own worth. The dressing gown on this famous patron of the arts and the garden accessories are not just everyday details, but objects that explain the essence of his independent character and charitable deeds. Behind the columns in the distance you can see the Orphanage building in Moscow for the upkeep of which Demidov donated large sums.

The portrait of Maria Alexeyevna Dyakova (1778) captivates one with its charming sitter who is so emotionally healthy and direct in showing her feelings. With remarkable ease and freedom the artist's brush moulds the form, conveys the play of light and shade and the fresh colours of the young face, and paints the soft rich hair and the silk and lace of the dress, amazing the viewer with the almost palpable textural beauty of this or that detail. On the reverse of the canvas are some moving lines by Count Segur relating to the sitter. "She is possessed of even more charm, than the brush could convey. And there is even more virtue in her heart, than beauty in her face." Her portrait, executed a few years later, shows signs of emotional strain and disillusion which can be sensed behind the outward aristocratic reserve of Dyakova-Lvova, who had by then concluded a secret marriage with the well-known poet and architect N.A. Lvov. Levitsky was friendly with many educat-

ed people of his day and for many years was in charge of the portrait class at the Academy of Arts.

Towards the end of the eighteenth century Russian sentimental prose and lyrical poetry developed under the influence of French literature and English verse, which had an impact on the artistic consciousness of the day. The cult of nature and the natural man ousted that of reason and civic virtue. Whereas enlightenment classicism extolled educated feelings, sentimentalism sang the praises of natural emotion. Sentimental features manifested themselves most clearly in the work of Vladimir Lukich Borovikovsky (1757–1825), particularly in his female figures. Born in the Ukraine, the artist received his early education from his father, an iconpainter. Moving to St Petersburg, he perfected his skill under the Austrian painter J.B. Lampi. His friendship with N.A. Lvov, V.V. Kapnist and G.R. Derzhavin influenced him greatly. The spiritual world of Borovikovsky's heroines is full of reverie and light melancholy. The new female fashions were free of excesses and emphasised elegant simplicity and naturalness. The landscape background with the motif of the country-house park, the low-cut dresses and hair styles of the sitters, and their informal, relaxed poses create a sense of freshness and inner harmony. The poetic theme of his portrait of the sister princesses Anna Gavrilovna and Varvara Gavrilovna Gagarina (1802) is the charm of tender female friendship and of making music at home.

The division into genres was completed by the end of the eighteenth century and landscape paint-

Dmitri Levitsky

Portrait of Maria Dyakova. 1778
Oil on canvas. 61 × 50

Vladimir Borovikovsky   →

*Portrait of Princesses Anna and
Varvara Gagarina.* 1802
Oil on canvas. 75 × 69.2

ing was now an independent sphere of art. Pride of place belonged to the "heroic" landscape, which depicted majestic panoramas from mountain or hill tops, waterfalls, lakes and ancient ruins. The stage-like structure of the composition with large trees at the edges, the precise distinction between fore- ground and background both in the drawing and in gradation of colour – from browns, through greens to the pale blue horizon – all this enhanced the dec- orative qualities of the landscape and its proximity to theatrical art forms. The leading master of this trend was Fyodor Mikhailovich Matveyev (1758–1826),

Fyodor Matveyev

View of Rome. The Coliseum. 1816
Oil on canvas. 135 × 194.3

whose work inclined towards the traditions of
Claude Lorrain and the German artist Jakob Phillipp
Hackert, his contemporary.

The canons of the classical landscape did not
remain supreme, however. In the canvases of Semyon
F.Shchedrin, who recorded views of the parks at
Pavlovsk and Gatchina, and the urban landscapes of
F.Ya. Alexeyev the lyrical element and concreteness
of what is depicted replaced the image structure of

the landscape genre. At the Tsar's request Fyodor
Yakovlevich Alexeyev (1753/1754?–1824) jour-
neyed round Russia with the aim of recording views
of Russian towns. His Moscow canvases are quite
unique. They reveal the artist's deep feeling for the
architectural image of Moscow before the fire of
1812 and his ability to convey the originality and
attraction of Russian mediaeval architecture.

Like the Napoleonic age in Europe, the reign of
Alexander I changed the political and cultural life of
Russia. The events of the war of 1812 against Napo-
leon greatly influenced the Russian view of life. New
trends in artistic consciousness and changes in the cri-

teria for evaluating art and its role in society promoted the formation of the romantic trend. The age of romanticism in Russia was not accompanied by a "Romantic battle" as in France. Nurtured in the Academy of Arts on classical aesthetic principles, the Russian romantics combined a heightened emotionality and expression of artistic image with a clear structure of form and balanced harmony of the whole. The Romantic works of O.A. Kiprensky, A.O. Orlovsky, K.P. Bryullov, A.G. Varneck, Sem. F. Shchedrin, V.E. Rayev and others coexisted with traditional academic art. This circle had flexible style limits, but invariably stood out for its treatment of themes and subjects.

Fyodor Alexeyev

View of the Resurrection and Nicholas gates and Neglinnaya Bridge from Tverskaya Street in Moscow. 1811
Oil on canvas. 78 × 110.5

Orest Kiprensky   →

Portrait of Alexander Pushkin. 1827
Oil on canvas. 63 × 54

Orest Kiprensky   →

Portrait of Daria Khvostova. 1814
Oil on canvas. 71 × 57.8

The cult of creativity, an awareness of the complexity of man's inner life greatly influenced the concept of the portrait. More than any other genre it reacted sensitively to the change in the social ideal. This also manifested itself in the flowering of the self-portrait. The new perception of the human personality in all its uniqueness can be seen with a special clarity and power in the art of Orest Adamovich Kiprensky (1782–1836), the most striking representative of Russian romanticism. His portrait of Daria Nikolayevna Khvostova (1814), which belongs to his early period, is full of consummate painterly skill and sensitivity to his sitter's inner world. The simple composition and natural pose with a slight tilt of the head convey the reserve and nobility of her character. There is gentleness and moral stamina in the facial features, the contemplative gaze and the flexible line of the mouth. The quivering mobility of the contours and the subtle colour combination of the olive background, the dark dress and the yellowish sand-coloured shawl lend the portrait a special elegance and charm. His portrait of the poet Alexander Sergeyevich Pushkin (1827) embodies the romantics' highest ideal, the creative individual endowed with the gift of transforming the world by the beauty and harmony of his poetic genius. Commissioned by Baron A.A.Delvig, the poet's friend, it became during Pushkin's lifetime a monument to this man who, in the opinion of his contemporaries, was worthy of "the triumphs of Petrarch and Tasso". In his turn Pushkin dedicated his famous poem "Suckling of the light-winged muse…" to the artist.

Another sphere where romantic trends were embodied was the landscape. The epic scale and elegiac aloofness of the 18th-century landscape were replaced by an interest in the effects of natural lighting and natural colour, unusual states of nature and genre motifs. Alongside the representation of natural elements, such as storms and blizzards, the themes of peace and quiet, man's fusion and harmony with nature, became widespread. In the canvases of Silvester F. Shchedrin and M.I. Lebedev nature is animated by the presence of man and his everyday labour and inspiration is ennobled by the beauty and majesty of nature. While retaining a classical clarity of style, Silvester Fyodosievich Shchedrin (1791–1830) brought to the Russian landscape fresh colour and radiant light, the vitality and beauty of nature and its inhabitants. Born in an artistic family and unusually talented, he was universally loved. Most of his short creative life was spent in Italy, Rome, Naples and Sorrento, whose picturesque views he recorded in many canvases with the true breadth and responsiveness of Russian talent.

A history painter, portraitist and the pride of the Academy of Arts, Karl Pavlovich Bryullov (1799–1852) was a master with a broad range of genres, from official, multi-figured canvases to everyday subjects and private sketches. His official canvases, while retaining the romantic elation of the portrait image, are executed with a colouristic brilliance suited to the artistic environment of palace and country-house interiors in the second quarter of the nineteenth century, in response to the new tastes of the Russian aristocracy. His *Lady on Horseback*

Silvester Shchedrin

*The Small Harbour at Sorrento with a View
of the Islands of Ischia and Procida* 1826
Oil on canvas. 45 × 60.7

(1832) is one of the finest specimens of portrait painting. The striking composition develops against an architectural landscape background, while the dramatis personae are united by a simple genre motif turned into a kind of festive spectacle. In such works as his portraits of N.V. Kukolnik (circa 1837), I.A. Krylov (1839) and A.N. Strugovshchikov (1840) the potential of Bryullov's realism, which combined an emotionally active image with apt and expressive characterisation, are most clearly realised. His *Self-Portrait* (1848), executed when the artist was already gravely ill, is a kind of late echo of romanticism in his later work. A certain deliberateness of pose and gesture that go back to the figures of Van Dyck and Rubens is relieved by the biographical concreteness of the work. The temperamental, broad painting seems to reflect the complex spiritual state of the artist, exhausted by the struggle against ill health and disappointment.

Karl Bryullov

Self-Portrait. 1848
Oil on cardboard. 64.1 × 54
(rounded top)

Karl Bryullov   →

Lady on Horseback. 1832
Oil on canvas. 291.5 × 206

The work of one of the most eminent masters of the nineteenth century, Alexander Andreyevich Ivanov (1806–1858) reflects the romantic trends in a special way. His painting *Apollo, Cyparissus and Hyacinthus Making Music and Singing* (1831–1834) personifies the very idea of creativity and contains a whole philosophy of art. Apollo, the focal point of the highest stage of inspiration, is listening to the timid playing of the young Hyacinthus. The three figures, like the three degrees on the path to perfection, are united in their shared meditation and music making. In selecting the famous statue of Apollo as a prototype, the artist sought to embody the spirit of Greek antiquity in the painting with the illusion of bring-ing antique plasticity to life. Romantic aesthetics, imbued with the desire for historicism, finds special embodiment in his painting of *Christ Appearing to the People (The Coming of the Messiah)*. In his search for a "universal subject" Ivanov chooses the New Testament event in which he sees the advent of a new world and the transfiguration of mankind. By aiming at recreating this ideal event with realistic means, the artist is following the new trends in art. Avoiding allegory, he seeks to convey the subject "with complete historical precision".

The philosophical turn of Ivanov's artistic think-ing is reflected in the complex relationship of the figures and their different psychological states. The

Alexander Ivanov

Olive Trees by Albano Cemetery. New Moon
Oil on canvas. 42.5 × 62.5

Alexander Ivanov   →

Apollo, Cyparissus and Hyacinthus Making Music and Singing. 1831–1834
Oil on canvas. 100 × 139.9

emergence of parallel themes and subject lines invests the painting with a variety of meanings: the world on the threshold of Christianity, the poetry of presentiments and expectations, the various emotions and levels of understanding what is taking place, the relationship between the different age groups. An important role in the creation of an authentic artistic image is played by the landscape. This explains why in his work on the painting,

Ivanov made a thorough study of each natural form capable of expressing the idea he had in mind. For Ivanov the action of the painting took place against the background of a landscape that included all the natural elements. Water and stones, a valley and mountains, soil and trees, foliage and sky – the relationship of these proto-elements of nature with their different physical material and form were investigated artistically with the help of nature stud-

Alexander Ivanov

*Christ Appearing to the People
(The Coming of the Messiah)*
1837–1857
Oil on canvas. 540 × 750

ies. His *Olive Trees by Albano Cemetery. New Moon* is one of the studies that the artist called "finished", meaning compositionally expressive and complete as a painting.

The beginning of the formation of the Moscow school of painting in the nineteenth century is connected with the work of Vasily Andreyevich Tropinin (1776–1857). For many years he was a serf and, due to a combination of circumstances, could not complete his education begun at the Academy of Art. He owes his skill largely to his independent and thoughtful work with nature. The words "Nature is the best teacher" express his main creative principle. While adhering to the academic system of consistent and multi-layered scumbling, Tropinin showed the originality of his talent in the special liveliness of the portrait image which he achieved with the help of simple but expressive devices and rich colour accents, whether he was depicting a slightly untidy feature of dress, such as the open collar of a shirt or a carelessly tied, brightly coloured neck scarf. His portrait of Arseny Vasilievich Tropinin (circa 1818), the artist's son, is one of the finest child's portraits in Russian art. As if taken unawares, the sitter reveals his finest qualities to the artist's observant and loving eye. The head portrayed close up in a slight turn and the rapid sideways glance create an impression of poetic duality, The young hero is in a world of his own and yet actively invites the spectator's attention. The canvas delights with its restrained colouring, strong brushwork, the inspired realism of the easily recognisable image ("There goes a serf boy…") and the child's

captivating gravity. The artist's decorative talent, his love of rich, bright colour can be seen in such works as *The Spinner* (late 1800s – early 1810s), *Portrait of K.G. Ravich* (1823) and *The Gold Embroidress* (1826). Tropinin's genre portraits were particularly popular. They reflected the world of ordinary people, which was new for art. The fine observation and accurate portrayal of the world of objects, musical instruments, tools and costume details were combined with an idealised image of the sitters. However, his portraits of city workers and artisans, works which were particularly dear to his heart, had yet to win the acclaim of art lovers. And his traditional idealisation of female sitters, which retained echoes of the "age of gallantry", made it easier for these characters to be included in the range of subjects and images worthy of art. The spectator could not fail to sense the artist's affection for these delightful figures, his deep respect and genuine interest in them.

The professional development of Alexei Gavrilovich Venetsianov (1780–1847) also took place outside the academic system of education. It was largely determined by his friendship with V.L. Borovikovsky, under whose guidance he made copies of classical works in the Hermitage. Absorbing the most diverse artistic impressions, Venetsianov advanced not only as an independent master, but also as the creator of the peasant genre, who was the first to introduce the world of Russian country folk into artistically convincing and poetic painting. The peasant's hard labour, seen through the prism of poetic perception, but not distorted by superficial

Vasily Tropinin
Portrait of Arseny Tropinin.
Circa 1818
Oil on canvas. 40.4 × 32

Vasily Tropinin

The Gold Embroidress. 1826
Oil on canvas. 81.3 × 63.9

Alexei Venetsianov

Spring Ploughing
First half of the 1820s
Oil on canvas. 51.2 × 65.5

idealisation, is presented as the everyday basis of popular life. Thus, the small canvas entitled *Spring Ploughing* (first half of the 1820s) together with *Summer Harvesting* (mid-1820s) form a kind of diptych covering the seasonal cycle of the peasant's life. Long before the flowering of the "landscape of mood" Venetsianov managed to convey the whole elusive yet simple charm of the Central Russian countryside animated by the "life and labours" of the Russian peasant. By assembling young talent around him and teaching according to his own pedagogical principles, Venetsianov brought to life a unique phenomenon in Russian culture, the artistic school that bears his name in the history of art. A.V. Tyranov, F.M. Slavyansky, G.V. Soroka and others enriched Russian art with their distinctive works. Thanks to Venetsianov's teaching the genre of the

interior developed in the 1820s and 1830s, which has recorded the harmonic, animated world of the country estate and its inmates.

New themes were introduced into genre painting by Pavel Andreyevich Fedotov (1815–1852), thanks to whom this genre was elevated to the level of great art. While still an officer he began to attend drawing classes at the Academy of Arts and soon gave up his military career. In a short time he not only acquired great skill, but also developed as an original master with his own theme and artistic vision. His work was not limited to social satire and extended beyond the framework of "moral-critical painting". *The Major Goes Courting* (1848), which became one of his most popular works, embodies the finest qualities of his painterly and compositional talent. To make the representation as natural as possible, the

Pavel Fedotov
Breakfast of an Aristocrat
1849–1850
Oil on canvas. 51 × 42

Pavel Fedotov   →
The Major Goes Courting
1848
Oil on canvas. 58.3 × 75.4

artist sought for charcters, costumes and domestic interiors in real life. The subject, based on the theme of the arranged marriage, is presented as a kind of theatrical mise-en-scene and, thanks to the artist's subtle direction, is rich in psychological nuances. Herein lies the distinctive feature of Fedotov's representational language. The situation of the "buying and selling" of the young bride and the resultant commotion in the merchant's family arouses a whole range of emotions in the bystanders, where simplicity and affectedness, pretence and honesty are revealed in the sharply characteristic and lively plasticity of the figures. While avoiding straightforward didacticism, Fedodov invests the scene with a special humour in which irony and mockery do not eliminate compassion and leniency.

The theme of vanity and pretence is present in most of the artist's works. The *Breakfast of an Aristocrat* (1849–1850) is based on a typical everyday subject revealing the habits of a young society man who is leading a double life. The small canvas impresses one with its precisely found psychological motif and brilliantly presented entourage. Through the motley "polyphony" of objects and things the artist reveals the vanity of this life of pretence and false respectability. As in *The Major Goes Courting* the canvas *Breakfast of an Aristocrat* impresses one with its authentic detail and the brilliance of the actual painting surface. Fedotov's art had no direct successors, but it influenced the subsequent development of genre painting, particularly that of the Moscow school.

Painting. Second Half of the 19th Century

LYUBOV ZAKHARENKOVA

The State Tretyakov Gallery possesses the most important and striking collection of Russian painting from the second half of the nineteenth century. The nucleus and pride of this collection are the works acquired by Pavel Mikhailovich Tretyakov (1832–1898), a Moscow merchant and industrialist and one of the finest men of his day. Having set himself the aim of "collecting the Russian school as it is in its consecutive development", for more than forty years (the first pictures were purchased in 1856) the founder of the Gallery followed the progress of contemporary artists, acquiring their works directly from the studio or at exhibitions. Tretyakov's organic connection with democratic culture, his civic standpoint and excellent taste determined the nature of his collecting. From a broad range of works he was able to select the best of what determined the progressive line in the artistic process.

The main idea that inspired Tretyakov's collecting was to create a museum of Russian art open to the general public, which would, to quote his own words, "be of benefit to many and bring pleasure to all."

Art of the second half of the nineteenth century is distinguished by great achievements in the artistic portrayal of the life of man and society, the Russian countryside and Russian history. It was during this period that the national school of realist painting emerged with special features largely determined by the complexity of Russia's social development and the intense spiritual searchings of the Russian intelligentsia.

The upsurge of social consciousness in Russia during the late 1850s and early 1860s led to reforms and the abolition of serfdom, to greater freedom for the individual. The legislator in art was still the Academy of Arts, which demanded imitation of models, as before, refusing to allow creative freedom. The desire of artists to cast off the fetters of old-fashioned ideas of artistic creativity led to the "revolt of the fourteen" who left the Academy because they were not allowed to choose their own subjects for the gold medal competition. This was the first open protest against dogmatism in art.

← Vasily Perov
Portrait of the Writer Fyodor Dostoyevsky. 1872
Oil on canvas. 99 × 80.5

In 1870 several well-known enthusiastic artists formed the Association of Travelling Art Exhibitions, which included all the best artistic talent of the day and became for many years to come the focal point of progressive ideas in art. These were seen as the rejection of imitation in art, the embodiment of true life in all its complexity and contradictions and the desire to depict urgent social and moral-ethical questions of the day. The very first exhibition of the Wanderers (the most common English translation of the Russian word *Peredvizhniki*, although "Itinerants" is also used) caused a sensation. Such paintings as *The Rooks Return* by A.K. Savrasov, *Peter the Great Interrogating Tsarevich Alexei Petrovich at Peterhof* by N.N. Ge, *Hunters Taking a Break* and the portrait of the writer A.N. Ostrovsky by V.G. Perov, and I.I. Shishkin's landscapes opened up new perspectives for the development of both genre and landscape painting, portraiture and history painting.

Realist painting in the second half of the nineteenth century had its own specific features at the various stages of its evolution. The 1860s were marked by the artist's urge to reveal the imperfections and contrasts of life. Pride of place at this time belonged to genre painting, which frequently tended to be highly critical. The 1870s were marked by a tendency towards more complex forms of depicting reality and the transition from negative pathos to the search for positive images in the life around. There was a flowering of the landscape and the portrait, the main hero of which was the creative individual, the bearer of spiritual values. .

In the 1880s and early 1890s Russian art reached the heights of great historical and philosophical generalisation. It began to reflect both the fate of individuals and the fate of the people as a whole. History painting acquired a special significance. For all the universality of striving and unity in the idea of transforming life through art, the work of each artist in this period is profoundly individual

Vasily Grigorievich Perov (1834–1882) became the head of the "denunciatory" trend in the 1860s. It was then that he created his finest genre works full of protest against the dark aspects of life, which were an insult to human dignity, and deep compassion for the suffering of the common people.

Perov's picture *The Last Tavern by the City Gate* (1868) is a masterpiece of Russian painting. By showing the outskirts of the town on a dark winter's evening, the sledges standing by a tavern called "The Parting", the little girl hunched up in the cold sitting in a sledge, the posts of the city gate bearing the Russian state emblem and the road beyond disappearing into endless expanses, the artist gives the painting an almost symbolic resonance. Through the dark subdued tones of the colouring he conveys a feeling of loneliness and discomfort. The picture is imbued with a sense of futile expectation and inescapable anguish.

In the 1870s Perov worked a great deal in the portrait genre. The general striving of Russian art at that time to acquire an ideal in reality made him turn to people who embodied the social conscience. His portrait of Fyodor Mikhaillovich Dostoyevsky (1872) commissioned by Pavel Tretyakov is one of

Vasily Perov

The Last Tavern by the City Gate. 1868
Oil on canvas. 51.1 × 65.8

the finest achievements not only of Perov, but of portraiture in the second half of the nineteenth century as a whole. The artist was able to recognise the great creative personality in Dostoyevsky and convey the image of a profound thinker, one of the finest men of his day. In her memoirs Anna Dostoyevskaya writes: "Before he began the portrait Perov visited us each day for a whole week; he found Fyodor Mikhailovich in different moods, chatted, provoked arguments and was able to note my husband's most characteristic facial expression, the one when he was immersed in his own literary thoughts. One might say that in his portrait Perov captured 'Dostoyevsky's moment of creativity'." The slightly hunched figure, the head drawn into the shoulders, the interlocked fingers of the clasped hands and the tense self-absorption – all this suggests a man with a tragic view of the world.

← Konstantin Flavitsky

Princess Tarakanova. 1863
Oil on canvas. 245 × 187.5

In his art Konstantin Dmitrievich Flavitsky (1830–1866) adhered to classical traditions, the principles bequeathed by K.P.Bryullov. His creative heritage is not extensive and he is known primarily as the author of the painting *Princess Tarakanova.* The work is based on a legend from Russian history according to which Princess Tarakanova, who said she was the daughter of Empress Elizabeth from her secret marriage to Count Alexei Razumovsky and laid claim to the Russian throne in Catherine the Great's reign, died in the Peter and Paul Fortress during the flood of 1777. Flavitsky depicts with great tragic power the suffering of this young woman facing certain death in a gloomy dungeon flooded with water, depicting her helplessness and despair most expressively.

In Russian realist painting of the second half of the nineteenth century a special place belongs to the landscape, in which to a greater extent than in other genres, it was possible to express a positive attitude to the world, the poetry of the natural elements in life. The desire to convey the quiet beauty of the Russian countryside in different seasons and states became the main task of artists.

Alexei Kondratievich Savrasov (1830–1897) was the first landscape painter of this period to introduce into art a new, deeply emotional attitude to nature. In his works simple, everyday motifs are turned into inspired images and an ordinary landscape is invested with subtle lyrical feeling.

The height of Savrasov's work is his picture *The Rooks Return* (1871). Painted for the most part in the village of Molvitino (Kostroma province), it is a generalized image containing some highly characteristic features of the Russian countryside and Russian life. This explains why it is often called a symbol of national landscape painting. The spectator sees a typical Central Russian landscape of gnarled birch trees, wooden houses, and a church, behind which open countryside recedes into the far distance. The dull grays of the departing winter are still present, but there is already a breath of spring in the air. The poetry of awakening life is conveyed beautifully. It lies in the tall tree trunks and thin branches of the birches, the rooks, those heralds of warm weather, who are busily renovating their nests, and the special luminescence of the paint texture. The fine drawing and delicate colour range of grayish-blue and gentle brown tones create a sense of the fluid, transitory character of this state of nature. Savrasov fills the canvas with anxious joy and trembling expectation. The artist also demonstrates his remarkable ability to sense the life of nature intuitively and see its vitalising influence on man.

In his landscape painting Fyodor Alexandrovich Vasiliev (1850–1873) combined a realistic perception of nature with a romantic attitude towards it. His works are remarkable for their originality and dynamism, as well as the vibrant use of colour.

A Wet Meadow (1872), executed in the Crimea when Vasiliev was already very ill with tuberculosis, was painted from memory with the use of sketches and studies made in Central Russia. The artist was striving to convey on canvas the state of nature that

← Alexei Savrasov

The Rooks Return. 1871
Oil on canvas. 62 × 48.5

Fyodor Vasiliev

A Wet Meadow. 1872
Oil on canvas. 70 × 114

follows a thunderstorm and heavy rain. He coped perfectly with this difficult task, imbuing the work with powerful emotion. What we see is a vast, rain-drenched meadow after a heavy storm has passed over it, with wet flattened grass and flowers. Everything is based on contrasting patches of ground some in shade, others lit by the sun which is coming out from behind a cloud. Most of the painting is taken up by the dynamic, multi-hued sky. We are reminded of the recent storm by a receding bluish-purple cloud driven away by the bright sun-light that is making the wet meadow shine and sparkle. The complexity and fine nuances of the colour structure and the light bluish haze create an impression of air filled with damp fragrance. We can sense the strong emotion of the artist who created this moving image of his native countryside when he was forced to be so far away from it.

← Ivan Shishkin
Pine Grove. Mast Timber
in Vyatka Province 1872
Oil on canvas. 113 × 164

The name of Ivan Ivanovich Shishkin (1832–1898) is associated with paintings of Russia's mighty forests and vast expanses. In his large canvases he reflected on an epic scale the riches of the Russian countryside, giant oaks, timber for building houses and ships. His infinite love of nature, tireless study of it and sharp powers of observation in respect of everything that grows out of the ground enabled him to create canvases in which the natural world appears in all its astounding variety, where each tree, bush and blade of grass has a life of its own and is depicted with great care and affection.

The painting *Pine Grove. Mast Timber in Vyatka Province* (1872) shows us the depth of the forest. As always with Shishkin, there is no rough detail here, everything is depicted with extreme care and precision. We can almost feel the thick needles of the mighty pines, the rough surface of the tree trunks and branches, the springy moss covering the ground, the cool water of the forest stream. The artist creates a powerful and fascinating image of the life of virgin forest, which is subject only to the laws of nature.

Ivan Nikolayevich Kramskoy (1837–1887) holds a special place in Russian art not only as an artist, thinker and eminent critic in the field of art but also as a figure who played an important role in artistic life. He was the initiator of the "revolt of the fourteen" and one of the organisers of the Association of Travelling Art Exhibitions, whose spiritual leader he remained for many years. His work embodies philo-

Ivan Kramskoy
Portrait of Pavel Tretyakov. 1876
Oil on canvas. 59 × 49

sophical reflections on life and the relationship of the individual and society. Kramskoy was a splendid portraitist. In this genre he showed a remarkably keen understanding of man and ability to express his essence.

Christ in the Wilderness (1872) is the artist's central work. Although linked with the Gospel account of the temptation of Christ in the wilderness, it does not aim to depict the story itself. The artist makes use of this subject as a kind of pretext for raising more general moral, philosophical questions relating to life in his day. It was Kramskoy's reflections on the need to make the choice between good and evil, his awareness of man's deep moral imperfections that gave him the idea of painting this work. Kramskoy's hero is not the Christ of the Gospel story engaged in a combat with the Devil and triumphing over him with meekness and words from Holy Scriptures. Kramskoy's Christ is a man suffering and oppressed by painful reflections. In seeking to embody his thoughts on the fate of the individual for whom Christian precepts are a measure of values, the artist creates a strict and laconic image, but one that is full of meaning. Here Kramskoy succeeds in conveying the extreme expenditure of spiritual force and torturous inner struggle of those who dare, in this world full of evil, "not to give way to evil one iota."

We should not be surprised to find a portrait of Pavel Tretyakov (1876) in Kramskoy's work. The artist and the collector were bound by many years of friendship and spiritual affinity. Tretyakov commissioned many of Kramskoy's portraits of celebrated Russian writers. Kramskoy in his turn gave Tretyakov a great deal of assistance with his collection. In his portrait of the Gallery's founder one can sense the richness of the inner world behind the grave exterior of this serious, sober-minded member of the merchant class. The inspired face with its fine features and intelligent eyes expresses great moral strength and dignity.

Nikolai Nikolayevich Ge (1831–1894) was also one of the founders of the Association of Travelling Art Exhibitions. He achieved a great deal in the sphere of the portrait and opened up new paths in the history genre, but above all he was known as the painter of canvases on New Testament subjects. Ge was not concerned with religious interpretation of the Gospel story. His interest in subjects from the life of Jesus provided the artist, who was given to deep reflection on the moral essence of human life, with the opportunity to express his attitude to many questions and events of his day.

In 1884 Ge produced a portrait of Count Lev Tolstoy. Tolstoy meant a great deal to the artist throughout his life. Ge was a great admirer of the writer and follower of his moral-philosophical teaching. Tolstoy is shown sitting at his desk in his Moscow mansion in Khamovniki at work on the manuscript of "What I Believe". Ge succeeded not only in recording the image of the great writer at work, but also in expressing his love and admiration of his talent. Tolstoy's complete absorption in what he is doing, his total concentration, enables the spectator to take a glimpse into the holy of holies in the writer's world – the birth of a new work. The writer's face seems to radiate light, like the sheets of paper on his desk, By creating such an impression of strength in the seated figure Ge is asserting the importance of Tolstoy's oeuvre and the power of his genius.

The painting *Golgotha* (1893) appeared during the artist's long period of work on the theme of the

Ivan Kramskoy

Christ in the Wilderness. 1872
Oil on canvas. 180 × 210

← Nikolai Ge

Portrait of Lev Tolstoy. 1884
Oil on canvas. 95 × 71.2

Crucifixion. Ge thought about depicting the Crucifixion for almost ten years, on and off, constantly deepening his understanding of its tragic significance. At one of the points in this search *Golgotha* appeared, a free interpretation of the New Testament events preceding the crucifixion. The spectator sees the terrible scene in which an invisible executioner's masterful hand calls for the sentence on Christ to be carried out. In the middle of the painting is Christ with the thieves who are also to be crucified on His right and left. The image of Christ appears as the embodiment of human suffering, pain for mankind and horror at the violence, cruelty and violation of truth that prevail in the world. The picture is unfinished and the colour, lighting and space are indicated roughly, yet even so it impresses one with its colossal tension and expressive pictorial language. The many different colour tones, the contrasts of light and shade and the dynamic sketchiness of the painting enhance even more the drama of what is taking place.

Vasily Vasilievich Vereshchagin (1842–1904) was not a member of the Association of Travelling Art Exhibitions, but was close to the Wanderers in the character of his work, which reflected his desire to achieve an objective recreation of reality. His main subjects were life in the East and the theme of war. Vereshchagin can hardly be called a painter of battle scenes, for his works contain no military storms or attacks, nor do they extol feats of valour and victories. What he conveys is not the outward aspect, but the "seamy side" of war, revealing its awful truth, cruelty and inhumanity.

In the picture *The Apotheosis of War* (1871), painted after several visits to Turkestan, the artist passes judgment in an extremely laconic, almost symbolical form, which nevertheless has a remarkably emotional impact, on war in general. The powerful artistic image created by Vereshchagin in this monumental canvas, which shows a heap of human skulls on scorched earth, the surroundings destroyed by fire, and traces of devastated towns, resounds like a terrible warning to this day. The inscription on the frame of the painting says: "Dedicated to all great conquerors, past, present and future."

In the genre painting of the second half of the nineteenth century an important place belongs to V.E. Makovsky, G.G. Myasoyedov, K.A. Savitsky, V.M. Maximov and N.A. Yaroshenko. Their work contains the most typical elements of Wanderers' genre painting, which developed productively in the 1870s and 1880s. In depicting individual, private scenes in the life of the different classes in town and country, genre painters frequently touched upon complex deep-rooted phenomena of Russian life.

Vladimir Yegorovich Makovsky (1846–1920) concentrated mainly on simple genre subjects which acquired the form of lively stories in his works. In transferring episodes from everyday life or ordinary people onto canvas, he portrayed them with compassion, affection, and occasionally humour and light irony.

Makovsky's painting *On the Boulevard* (1886–1887) is one of the artist's finest creations. It shows a young couple sitting on a bench in a boulevard of

Nikolai Ge   →

Golgotha. 1893
Oil on canvas. 222.4 × 191.8

Vasily Vereshchagin

The Apotheosis of War. 1871
Oil on canvas. 127 × 197

Vladimir Makovsky

On the Boulevard
1886–1887
Oil on canvas. 53 × 68

Konstantin Savitsky   →

Repair Work on the Railway. 1874
Oil on canvas. 100 × 175

a large city. The man holding the accordion has left the village to find seasonal employment in the town. The woman with the young child is his wife, who has come up from the village to visit her husband. The spectator is now a witness to this far from happy scene. The young woman's feelings encounter the carefree attitude of her indifferent husband, who has grown used to city life and is almost a stranger to his family. They are sitting side by side, but are miles apart. The image of the despondent woman is particularly expressive. The coldish tones of the urban landscape add to the overall mood of poignant sadness.

Genre painting in the 1870s and 1880s was characterised by works with a complex composition, a detailed subject and a large number of figures. V.V.Stasov called them "choral" paintings. One of these painters was Konstantin Apollonovich Savitsky (1844–1905). The main theme of his work was peasant life. "Choral" painting enabled Savitsky to depict broad layers of peasant life as a whole, instead of individual characteristic images and isolated typical facts and phenomena.

His *Repair Work on the Railway* (1874) is one such work. The artist shows peasants who having recently gained their freedom from serfdom are now victims of new forms of oppression, and continue to bear the brunt of backbreaking physical toil. The theme of exhausting, monotonous labour that

brings no joy is the picture's main message. It is expressed in the grim faces and frequently repeated identical movements of the figures.

Paintings on subjects from peasant life also predominated in the work of Vasily Maximovich Maximov (1844–1911). A peasant by birth, with a first-hand knowledge of country life, he managed to reflect in his pictures both the hard lot of the peasant and the poetry of patriarchal peasant life with its traditions and customs.

In *All in the Past* (1889) the artist depicts the neglect and ruin of country estates in Russia after the abolition of serfdom. By the wing of a small country house we see the elderly lady of the house

reminiscing nostalgically about the past to her old servant who is hunched up over her knitting. In the background is the house with its windows boarded up. The former prosperity of these "nests of the gentry" is gone forever and their special customs, the distinctive pattern of the life of the gentry on their country estates, is now a thing of the past.

Many aspects of Russia's complex social life in the late 1870s and 1880s, such as the appalling conditions of the workers, the People's Will movement, the student unrest and the humiliating position of women who lacked all rights, were reflected in the work of that striking member of the Wanderers Nikolai Alexandrovich Yaroshenko (1846–1898).

Vasily Maximovich Maximov

All in the Past. 1889
Oil on canvas. 72 × 93.5

His life as an artist began rather late. He served for many years in the army, but eventually his love of art decided his future path.

In his portrait of the actress Pelageya Antipievna Strepetova (1884), who played many of the tragic roles in A.N.Ostrovsky's plays on the Russian stage,

Yaroshenko shows not so much the actress as a woman with a sensitive, vulnerable soul who somehow personifies the pain and suffering of Russian women in general. Her inner world is revealed in the simplicity of her appearance, her bright sad gaze, which is full of silent reproach and at the same time trust in people.

The work of Ilya Yefimovich Repin (1844–1930) is associated with the greatest achievements of Russian realism. His brilliant talent and the tremendous scope of his art won him fame as the most celebrated Russian artist. His range of themes and images is unusually broad and diverse. He created history, genre and portrait works and also frequently turned to the landscape.

The broad coverage of all aspects of Russian life found in Repin's work and its revealing social and psychological features are seen most clearly in his *Religious Procession in Kursk Province* (1880–1883). The painting was executed after a visit by Repin to Kursk and the surrounding area where the famous religious processions with the miracle-working icon of Our Lady of Kursk took place each summer and autumn. The canvas depicts one of these processions. Here we see practically the whole of provincial Russia, its different social strata. In the middle of the procession are the landowners, merchants, clergy and military. This group is led by the woman carrying the miracle-working icon, who radiates a strong sense of her own importance. Her haughty self-confidence conveys most eloquently the attitude of the powers-that-be, whose security is vigilantly protected by the constables and headmen with the help of sticks and lashes. In front of the procession some sturdy peasants stride sedately, followed by two women who are carrying the icon's empty case with great care and servility. Here too are the officials and choristers. The painting is remarkable for the variety of types, faces, poses, movements and gestures of the motley, colourful crowd of people. While striving to convey the grandiose magnificence of the procession, the artist has no wish to omit his negative observations and reflections on life. There is hardly a single person in the painting who reflects the light of true faith and

Nikolai Yaroshenko

Portrait of the Actress
Pelageya Strepetova. 1884
Oil on canvas. 120 x 78

prayerful communion with what is taking place. The crowd includes an archdeacon in his bright festive robes holding a censor, yet the artist finds nothing spiritual in his figure either. In the left-hand section of the procession we see poor people, beggars and pilgrims. The most striking image in this group is the hunchback who believes with all his heart and soul and is limping forward eagerly. The inner beauty and spirituality transforming his features stand out against the crowd of arrogant, indifferent or apathetic faces. Only in this suffering creature has the artist expressed the purity and sincerity of true faith.

With the development of critical realism history painting underwent some important changes. It was reformed by the distinguished artists N.N. Ge, I.E. Repin and, in particular, V.I. Surikov. In their canvases they sought to resurrect the spirit of historical events, to record in artistic images the real contradictions of bygone ages, to recreate concrete historical figures with all their characteristics, destinies, passions and collisions.

The work of Vasily Ivanovich Surikov (1848–1916) marks the height of Russian history painting in the second half of the nineteenth century. In turning to the critical stages in Russian history, the

Ilya Repin

Religious Procession in Kursk Province. 1880–1883
Oil on canvas. 175 × 280

Ilya Repin

Tsarevna Sofia Alexeyevna after a year's imprisonment in Novodevichy Convent, during the execution of the Streltsy and the torturing of her servants in 1698. 1879
Oil on canvas. 201.8 × 145.3

artist was conscious of history as a drama and revealed a deep understanding of national character. At the same time he possessed a rich plastic talent, thanks to which his works make a most powerful emotional impact.

In the painting *The Morning of the Streltsy's Execution* (1881) Surikov depicts an event in the reign of Peter the Great connected with the revolt of the Streltsy against Peter's reforms. The artist depicts the moment before the execution of the Streltsy, treating the scene as the clash of two forces. The first seems to include the whole element of popular life, the disorderly crowd of Streltsy, their wives and children and the people who have gath-

ered in the square. The second consists of Peter himself, the ambassadorial corps and men of the new regular army, the Preobrazhensky regiment. The main theme of the painting is revealed in the confrontation between the red-bearded Strelets and Peter, who are glaring at each other with irreconcilable hostility. Each believes in his own cause: for the Strelets it is mediaeval Russia and the rebellious,

Vasily Surikov

The Morning of the Streltsy's Execution. 1881
Oil on canvas. 218 × 379

Detail   →

long-suffering Russian people, for Peter it is the new Russia about to be born and the relentless power of the state. This painting was the first in which Surikov revealed the full power of his historical vision. The artist knew that at critical moments in history the relationship between the authorities and the people grows more strained than ever and that in this confrontation the full burden of historical collisions is borne by the people. The artistic treatment here is truly polyphonic. Surikov makes use of the full arsenal of representational devices. He achieves expressiveness not only with the help of striking imagery, but also by using a highly dramatic system of lines and forms, uniting the polyphony of the painting's compositional, rhythmic and colour structure into a single whole.

Viktor Mikhailovich Vasnetsov (1848–1926) belonged to the generation of Wanderers whose

← Vasily Surikov

Menshikov in Berezovo. 1883
Oil on canvas. 169 × 204

Viktor Vasnetsov

*After the Battle of Igor, son of Svyatoslav,
with the Polovtsians.* 1880
Oil on canvas. 205 × 390

work marked the beginning of the transition from critical realism to the search for new content and new formal devices. Vasnetsov found his own way in art through the acquisition of new pictorial images. He turned to the language of folklore and ancient traditions and was one of the founders of the new "national" trend in Russian art; working as he did in different art forms, he became the creator of the Neo-Russian style.

His painting *After the Battle of Igor, son of Svyatoslav, with the Polovtsians* (1880) is based on the subject of the "Lay of Igor's Host". It shows the battlefield after the battle of the Russians against the Polovtsians. The vast steppe is strewn with the bodies of dead warriors. Birds of prey circle overhead and a blood-red moon is rising. The powerful spiritual force of the old Russian epic with its patriotic fervour finds fitting embodiment in Vasnetsov's

monumental canvas. Using devices characteristic of folklore the artist tones down the tragedy of the event, imbuing the canvas with an epic spirit. In the centre of the composition are the fallen warriors whom the artist deliberately idealises, extolling the strength and bravery of the Russian men who laid down their lives for their country. By rejecting the concrete and real in favour of the folkloric and poetic, Vasnetsov succeeded in conveying on this canvas the faith in the greatness of the people and their mighty strength which is contained in the "Lay".

In his landscape painting Arkhip Ivanovich Kuindji (1842?–1910) combined adherence to the romantic tradition with realism and epic breadth in the portrayal of nature. He was attracted by motifs that would help him achieve unusual light effects.

In his search for new ways of portraying moonlight or strong sunlight hitherto unknown in Russian painting, he occasionally invested real images with a mysterious aura and fantastic colouring that generates strong poetic feelings.

In the painting *The Birch Grove* (1879) Kuindji conveys the effect of glorious dazzling sunlight. In resorting to colour and light contrasts, the artist is searching for a new artistic language. A certain conventionality in the compositional structure makes the painting resemble a stage set. Detailed reproduction of nature is replaced by generalised representation of objects, and careful working of tonal transitions gives way to the silhouette and large planes of colour. These devices found by Kuindji anticipate the decorative experiments of Russian artists at a later period.

← Arkhip Kuindji

The Birch Grove. 1879
Oil on canvas. 97 × 181

Vasily Polenov

A Moscow Courtyard. 1878
Oil on canvas. 64.5 × 80.1

The work of Vasily Dmitrievich Polenov (1844–1927), particularly his finest landscapes and genre paintings, reflect his search for beauty and harmony in life and nature.

A Moscow Courtyard (1878) is one of his greatest works. In depicting this everyday scene in a typical Moscow courtyard, the artist has managed to fill the picture with a radiant sense of joy and happiness in ordinary things. Simply and with great affection Polenov shows the inhabitants of this small corner of Moscow, the familiar rhythm of their life which seems to have dissolved in the serene calm of the sunlit courtyard. In seeking to convey his direct impressions of this contact with nature, Polenov was the first Russian artist to make such free and open use of the devices of plein-air painting, filling the landscape with light and air. By striving for a harmonious colour structure, immersing objects in an airy haze and softening the brightness of the colours, he creates a poetic world full of beauty and tranquility. The rich and subtle combination of green with white, silver and pale blue gives the painting a festive note.

The finest landscape painting of the 1880s and 1890s is connected with the name of Isaak Ilyich Levitan (1860–1900). A pupil of Savrasov and Polenov, he inherited many of the finest qualities in their art. His sensitive feelings and ability to record with artistic devices the constantly changing states of the human soul in relation to the life of nature enable us to call Levitan an artist of the landscape of mood. In his world outlook he inclined towards the new generation of Russian painters, but his adher-

Isaak Levitan

Golden Autumn. 1895
Oil on canvas. 82 × 126

ence to realism for depicting scenes of nature shows his deep links with the art of the Wanderers.

The large canvas *Above Eternal Rest* (1894) expresses Levitan's meditations on life and death, human destiny, and the loneliness of the human soul amid the vastness of the universe. Into the broad expanse of a lake under an endless sky juts the tip of a promontory with a tiny church and a graveyard. A light in the church window is the only reminder of man. The heavy thunderclouds advancing relentlessly and about to swallow up the bright patch of sky combined with the tiny vulnerable piece of land and its forgotten graves strike a tragic note that fills the whole picture.

In many of its works the realistic art of the Wanderers, basically sincere and authentic, expressed the thoughts and feelings of the finest people of the day addressed to the public at large. The sense of disharmony between man and society, the disparity between the life around them and the ideal life, encouraged some artists "to present people with a mirror that would make their hearts sound the alarm" (to quote Kramskoy) and others to affirm the noble elements in nature and man. Their art still has something very precious and important to say to the people of today.

Isaak Ilyich Levitan

Above Eternal Rest. 1894
Oil on canvas. 150 × 206

Mikhail Nesterov

The Young Bartholomew's Vision. 1889–1890
Oil on canvas. 160 × 211

Painting. Late 19th to the early 20th century

MARIA ZINGER-GOLOVKINA

The State Tretyakov Gallery has one of the largest collections of Russian painting from the late 19th to the early 20th century. Continuing the collections of mediaeval Russian art and Russian painting of the 18th and 19th centuries, it constitutes a special page in the Russian cultural heritage, a qualitatively new stage in its development.

The period of the late 19th and early 20th century, a turning point in the history of Russian art, is frequently called a renaissance. The work of the Wanderers laid the foundation for experiments by a new generation of artists, but genre realism and social analysis of Russian reality could no longer cope with the complex and problems presented by the 20th century. Scientific discoveries, the broad assimilation of the world's cultural heritage and the national past led to a global rethinking of the criteria for artistic creativity and a re-evaluation of generally accepted ideas. The breakdown of dividing lines between the different art forms and genres, the emergence of the idea of universal synthesis, and an intense interest in the secrets of professional mastery, in plumbing the depths of the creative ego, demanded the creation of new artistic means and plastic devices for understanding the new and complex picture of the world. Light and sound increasingly became the focal point of the artist's attention.

In the 1880s and 1890s, the principles of impressionism with its cult of the instantaneous and immediate became increasingly evident in Russian painting and sculpture, as well as music and to some extent architecture By the turn of the century the desire to embrace the world in its eternal and unchanging entirety and take a look into the unknown had produced the aesthetic trends of symbolism and neo-romanticism. The idea of the organic rhythmical connection of different aspects of being was pivotal in the stylistic experiments in the age of art nouveau.

The period from the 1890s to 1910s produced a whole galaxy of painters who determined the broad spectrum of Russian artistic life with its variety of trends and groupings. The works of M.V. Nesterov, M.A. Vrubel, V.A. Serov, K.A. Korovin, A.N. Benois, K.A. Somov, V.E. Borisov-Musatov, F.A. Malyavin, N.K. Roerich, B.M. Kustodiev, A.Ya. Golovin, S.Yu. Sudeikin, N.N. Sapunov, P.V. Kuznetsov, M.S. Sariyan and others bear visual testimony to the intense artistic and philosophical searching that took place in Russian art during the late 19th and early 20th century.

One of the first paintings of this period acquired by Pavel Tretyakov was *The Young Bartholomew's Vision* (1889–1890) by Mikhail Vasilievich Nesterov (1862–1942). In the same year, 1890, it made a great impression on his contemporaries at an exhibition of the Association of Travelling Art Exhibitions.

The appearance of the mysterious monk to the young Bartholomew (the future Sergius of Radonezh,

founder of the Trinity-St Sergius monastery) and his prophesy of the boy's great spiritual mission is an episode taken from the "Life of the Venerable Sergius" compiled by Sergius' pupil, Epithanius the Wise. The countryside around Abramtsevo, not far from the Trinity monastery, where this picture was painted, acquires the generalized features of a Central Russian landscape with a small church on a hill. The naïve purity of the young Bartholomew and the radiant spirituality of the countryside symbolize Holy Russia. This quiet scene gives the viewer a vivid sense of the miraculous vision.

The world of legend, folk tales, epic verse and fairy stories was a key element in the experiments of the Abramtsevo circle which, at the turn of the 20th century, united such leading artists as M.V. Nesterov, M.A. Vrubel, V.M. Vasnetsov, V.A. Serov and K.A. Korovin. Set up by the patron S.I. Mamontov on his estate at Abramtsevo, it became a focal point in the 1880s and 1890s for the most important aesthetic experiments, particularly the national-romantic searching of the age of art nouveau with its urge for stylistic unity that broke down the barriers between art and life, the everyday and the infinite.

These ideas culminated in the work of Mikhail Alexandrovich Vrubel (1856–1910), who subsequently became the personification of the neoromantic image of the master creator. The symbolist dream of the omnipotence of Art and Beauty was dramatically embodied in this artist's personality.

← Mikhail Vrubel

Demon (Seated). 1890
Oil on canvas. 116.5 × 213.8

Mikhail Vrubel

Lilac. 1900
Oil on canvas. 160 × 177

Valentin Serov   →

Girl with Peaches. 1887
Oil on canvas. 91 × 85

Longing for "the music of the integrated individual" is the inner key to his famous *Demon (Seated)* (1890). The mighty, fractured forms embody, to quote Vrubel's own words, "a spirit not so much evil as suffering and grieving, yet at the same time masterful […] and majestic." The powerful torso with the tensely clasped hands seems constricted by the narrow band of the canvas, and the figure's elemental strength restrained by the crystals of fantastic blossoms. The face possesses an infernal majesty together with human vulnerability. Focused on the eternal secrets of nature, the Demon's gaze strains into the distance, where the purplish-gold "magma" of the sunset rends the darkness of the sky. The unusual mosaic of luminescent brushstrokes creates the image of an elevated, poetic world.

At the turn of the century the motifs of crystal, stone, wood, a river, a shell or a flower became some of the most characteristic elements of the new synthetic style of art nouveau. They embodied, as it were, the hidden, personified soul of nature and the things around it. In Vrubel's *Lilac* (1900) the glimmering of the deep bluish-red tones and the "lilac dusk" of night, heavy with aromatic blossom, sweeps over the spectator like waves. The pale contours of a timid girl's face, which embodies the delicate impermanence, the undeveloped "soul", of the lilac, rise from a mass of expressive brushstrokes as if from sea foam. The artist has deliberately chosen a large, almost square format, thereby giving the canvas the appearance of a monumental decorative panel.

The artists of the Ambramtsevo circle arrived at the affirmation of beauty and human harmony with the world by different paths.

The work of Valentin Alexandrovich Serov (1865–1911) reflects the most important stages in the development of Russian art of the late 19th and early 20th century with its new plastic discoveries.

"I want to paint joyful things", the young Serov announced. His Abramtsevo portrait of Vera Mamontova, *Girl with Peaches* (1887) amazed people with its freshness and innovation. Everything about it was unprecedented: the interior full of light and air with a window facing the garden, the subtle colour relationships, the bold fragmentation of the foreground, the table with the peaches, and above all the barely restrained liveliness of the restless, swarthy faced girl sitting at the table, her attentive gaze fixed on the viewer. The illusion of being present achieved here draws the viewer into a quiet, silent dialogue. This captured moment becomes an immortal image of youth.

A future master of the character portrait, Serov creates a special "picture" image here, a kind of portrait of "condition", one might say. This portrait and the following one of his *Girl in Sunlight* (1888) heralded the advent of a new method in Russian painting – impressionism.

The Rape of Europa panel (1901) painted by Serov following a journey to Greece with Leon Bakst sums up, as it were, his search for a synthetic "grand" style. The artist seems to remove centuries of stratification from the Creto-Mycenaean myth of

Valentin Serov

The Rape of Europa. 1910
Oil on canvas. 71 × 98

the seduction of the young Phoenician princess Europa by the god Zeus in the form of a bull, revealing the timeless freshness and poetry of the ancient legend. As if anticipating the interest of future painters in the archaic and primitive, he reduces the naïve conventionality of his new painterly manner to extreme laconicism. The centricity of the composition on the square canvas, the rhythmical repetition of the curves in the rippling of the ploughed up surging swell, the backs of the diving dolphins and, finally, the princess's precarious pose all create an image full of vital power and delicate beauty.

The Rape of Europe was one of the last manifestations of the monumental decorative experiments of art nouveau. At the very source of these experiments we find Serov's friend Konstantin Alexeyevich

Korovin (1861–1939), painter, author of architectural projects and one of the founders of the neo-Russian style and Russian painterly impressionism. In the free atmosphere of the Abramtsevo circle his talent for improvisation, the main method of impressionism, soon unfolded. His method developed most fully in Paris, however, which later became the artist's final refuge. Korovin's rich colours and pastose palette and his habit of painting in a single session, "a la prima" were regarded by his contemporaries as a sign of the new dynamic consciousness of the emergent twentieth century. In his *Paris. Boulevard des Capucines* (1911) the huge, noisy city is seen slightly from above, in sharp foreshortening and a stream of iridescent light. Korovin, who remained true all his life to his direct, impres-

Konstantin Korovin

Paris. Boulevard des Capucines. 1911
Oil on canvas. 65 × 80.7

sionistic perception of nature, enriches it with his impulsive energy, artistry and experience as a celebrated stage designer.

The theatre is one of the most important trends that united the efforts of a whole series of leading Russian masters at this time. At different periods stage design attracted V.D. Polenov and M.A. Vrubel, K.A. Korovin and V.A. Serov, N.K. Roerich and A.N. Benois, N.N. Sapunov and S.Yu. Sudeikin, A.Ya. Golovin and K.F. Yuon.

The main bearer of the ideas of stage design at the turn of the century was the St Petersburg World of Art association. It appeared in 1898 on the initiative of Sergei Diaghilev, the future organiser of the world famous Saisons Russes, and Alexander Benois, with the aim of uniting the new experi-

ments in various art forms. "Grass-roots" questing was replaced by the systematic mastery of the traditions of West European art seen through the prism of nostalgic, sometimes grotesque or idyllic pictures of the past. The World of Art members focused on images of the "age of gallantry" in the 17th and 18th centuries of French baroque and rococo with their courteous manners, harmonic architectural ensembles and regular parks and gardens.

One of the manifestations of the new stylistic universality in the work of the World of Art was to be found in book and journal illustration, as well as easel graphics. *An Italian Comedy. The Love Letter* (1905) by Alexander Nikolayevich Benois (1870–1960) is very close to a painting in its compositional treatment. In depicting a theatre performance, the artist

Alexander Benois

An Italian Comedy.
The Love Letter. 1905
Gouache and watercolour
heightened with white
on paper mounted on
cardboard. 49.6 × 67.4

Konstantin Somov   →

Lady in Blue. 1897–1900
Oil on canvas. 103 × 103

makes clever use of the "wings" construction of space and the frontal contrast of foreground and background, while retaining a sense of the flat surface of the paper The contrasting light and shade and the linear expressiveness of the silhouettes unite the musicians in the foreground with the actors at the back of the stage and subordinate the folkloric informality of the Italian "comedia del'arte" to the logic of rhythmical resonances.

The work of Konstantin Andreyevich Somov (1869–1939) is a vivid illustration of the portraiture achievements of the World of Art. His portrait of the artist E.M. Martynova, which has gone down in the history of Russian art as the *Lady in Blue* (1897–1900), is more than just a fine psychological characterization. Somov's contemporaries had good reason to call him an "enchanter". The sitter's out-

stretched hand with a book reminds one of the stylistics of formal portraiture in the 18th and early 19th centuries. This sadly trusting, yet enigmatic gesture touches a chord, as it were, in the empty, symbolical park surrounding the figure of the woman, where the artist has even depicted himself. The "Echo of Time Past" is the name given by the artist to another female portrait now in the Tretyakov Gallery. Somov was one of the representatives of Russian "retrospectivism" with its nostalgia for the lost "golden age", the spirit of Russian stately homes and their idyllic, patriarchal and spectral poetry of bygone days.

The cosy "nests of the gentry" depicted by Maria Vasilievna Yakunchikova-Veber (1870–1902) are imbued with the meditative poetry of solitude. She spent most of her life abroad and died young. Her

Maria Yakunchikova-Veber

From a Window of the Old House. Vvedenskoye. 1897
Oil on canvas. 88.3 × 106.5

paintings with their painfully subdued colouring contain notes of deep romantic suffereing. *From a Window of the Old House. Vvedenskoye* (1897) shows the pale light of dawn reflected in the river through various details and draws the viewer's gaze beyond the distant empty horizon.

The world of the Russian country estate was also a source of inspiration for Igor Emmanuilovich Grabar (1871–1960), painter, architect, theoretician and art historian, as well as trustee and later director of the Tretyakov Gallery. Other images and pictorial tendencies also appear in his work, however. In the deliberately fragmentary nature of his landscapes and country house interiors and in his special, analytically separate brushstrokes we find

plastic experiments characteristic of the early 1900s. The image of spring renewal of the world, particularly popular in Russia at the turn of the century, is the leitmotif of his famous *February Azure* (1904). The spring birch trees appear in the transparent aureole of the azure sky and sparkling, iridescent rays. His contemporaries regarded this picture as a kind of manifesto of a new stage in the impressionist vision of the world.

The development of the traditions of Russian impressionism and the devices for conveying spatial light and air (plein air) was an important trend in the activity of the Moscow Union of Russian Artists which arose in 1903. While continuing the aesthetic endeavours of the Wanderers and the Abramtsevo

Igor Grabar

February Azure. 1904
Oil on canvas. 151 × 84

circle, the Union of Russian Artists became a focal point for the national-romantic experiments of the 1900s and 1910s.

A new landscape vision united the various pictorial genres, from the historical to the genre portrait, the interior and the still life. Natural freshness and immediacy of perception is combined with decorative conventionality and monumental image treatment. Rhythmic generalisation of the silhouette, emphatic relief of the texture, and a large format were signs of the new stylistic approach.

The main thing now was not so much a narrative subject, as the general mood, motif, or atmosphere of what was depicted. A pastose impressionistic manner conveys the inner beauty of everyday life in the paintings of A.E. Arkhipov, S.A. Vinogradov, L.V. Turzhansky and S.Yu. Zhukovsky. The world of the Russian countryside is depicted not so much as gloomy, backbreaking toil, but as the rich life of nature. Artists are increasingly attracted by the soundness of patriarchal customs.

The hidden poetry of being, subtle light and air perspective, rich colour nuances and a barely perceptible touch of stylization make the viewer an active participant in the painting *A Wedding Procession in Moscow (17th century)* by Andrei Petrovich Ryabushkin (1861–1904),. While remaining true to the details of this distant, pre-Petrine age, its dress, architecture and customs, the artist concentrates on the play of spatial levels: his figures, somewhat stiff as in mediaeval Russian icons, merge into a single harmonic and lyrical chorus. Born in a Russian vil-

lage, Ryabushkin imbues his works with complex, ritual musicality.

The epic, fairy-tale intonation of A.M. Vasnetsov's landscapes and the colourful heroes of S.V. Ivanov show a keen interest in the patriarchal life of pre-Petrine Russia, Muscovy. The Wanderers' favourite subjects of the homeland and the common people are now enriched with new folkloric images and an attempt to depict the national flavour of Russian artistic culture.

F.A. Malyavin's *Whirlwind* (1906) is an explosive dance that whips up the vast surface of the canvas (more than two by four metres) into a fiery sea of calico, out of which the dusky faces of women rise as if from a whirlwind. Filipp Andreyevich Malyavin (1869–1940), an icon-painter from Mount Athos of peasant stock, became for his contemporaries a daring pictorial experimenter. The artist boldly transfers the devices of monumental decorative art onto the canvas. His rich colour range and powerful

mosaic-like brushwork produce a festive, although disturbing image of this ecstatic outburst, which unites movement, bewitchment, grotesque and the epic breadth of folklore. Painted in 1906 at the height of the peasants' revolutionary activity, the painting was seen by contemporaries as an historical work. In the same year it was purchased by the Gallery and Malyavin, a member of the Union of Russian Artists, was awarded the title of academician.

The theme of popular festivities receives a different treatment in the canvases of another painter close to the Union of Russian Artists, Konstantin Fyodorovich Yuon (1875–1958). A master of architectural composition, in the painting *A Village Festival. Tver gubernia* (1910) Yuon makes the white vertical of a bell-tower an integral part of this bright impressionistic landscape with groups of people in their Sunday best standing round it. His precise natural observations are full of hidden rhythmic expression, a sense of the folkloric. Yuon, who also tried

← Andrei Ryabushkin

A Wedding Procession in Moscow (17th century). 1901
Oil on canvas. 90 × 206.5

Filipp Malyavin

Whirlwind. 1906
Oil on canvas. 223 × 410

his hand at stage design, brings to the atmosphere of popular festivities some subtle, barely perceptible scenic devices, giving it the flavour of a bright, thronging spectacle.

In the late 1900s and early 1910s the creative experiments of the Union of Russian Artists and the World of Art revealed more and more points of contact, particularly in the sphere of stage design with its interest in historical and national-romantic problems.

The experiments with imagery by the World of Art in this period are seen most consistently in the work of Alexander Yakovlevich Golovin (1863–1930), the painter and outstanding stage designer, whose sketches were used by Yuon for Diaghilev's 1908 Paris production of the opera "Boris Godunov" with Fyodor Chaliapin in the main role.

Golovin's portrait painted in the same year of Chaliapin as Holofernes in A.N.Serov's opera "Judith" is an important late manifestation of the art nouveau style. The artist focuses attention on the singer's gestures that reveal the depth of human nature. The fearsome king besotted with the wily Judith is shown in the whole gamut of emotions that hold him in thrall. The loose robes, the cup and the light against the background of sumptuous oriental drapery reproduce the makeup, costumes and sets for the opera designed by V.A. Serov. At the same time the profile treatment of the figure reclining on the royal couch and the powerful gesture of the theatrically outstretched hand remind one of an Assyro-Babylonian bas-relief. The spare decorative ornamental forms moulded with broad, dryish brushstrokes in a monochrome ochre range make this panel resemble a fresco, subjecting the singer's almost demonic expression to strict and majestic monumental rhythm.

The search for a "grand" style is the distinctive feature of the World of Art as revived in 1910. Its chairman that year was Nikolai Konstantinovich Roerich (1874–1947), artist, archaeologist, historian and designer for Diaghilev's Saisons Russes.

The composition *Visitors from Overseas* (1901), which sums up, as it were the artist's journey along the Great Waterway "from the Varangians to the Greeks", is one of Roerich's most important works on the theme of Old Russia and the Slavic peoples and was suggested to him by Pavel Tretyakov.

A fairy-tale "remote" Russia is seen through the eyes of Varangian travellers from overseas. The artist enhances the powerful foreground with the approaching Scandinavian vessels. The epic narrative quality and colourful woodcut (*lubok*) forms merely heighten the illusion of historical authenticity of this picturesque "story", the clashing shields, flapping sails, and seagulls cries in expectation of a festive trading fair. In the hands of Roerich the symbolist, this everyday scene represents the meeting of two great, but different worlds: the militant Varangians and the enigmatic Slavs, who are not visible to the viewer. Painted at the Paris studio of the well-known populariser of prehistoric times, the monumental artist Fernand Cormon, Roerich's picture became one of the programme manifestations of the general interest at that time in the ancient origins of human civilisation.

Archaic motifs were particularly popular from the mid-1900s among artists close to the revived

Alexander Golovin

A Portrait of Fyodor Chaliapin as Holofernes. 1908
Tempera and pastel on canvas. 163.5 × 212

World of Art. In the painting *Sea Shore* (1907) by Konstantin Fyodorovich Bogayevsky (1872–1943), the bard of austere Crimean landscapes, fragments of southern scenery are crystallised into an image of the mysterious Cimmeria, the repository of ancient, including antique, traditions. The artist's conventional manner has united in a single whole clusters of clouds, the terrible waves crashing against the cliffs and the fused forms of fortresses, treated in restrained, subdued, powdery colours, which make the painted surface of the canvas resemble the texture of a woven tapestry.

Boris Mikhailovoch Kustodiev (1878–1927), one of the most "entertaining" painters of the late 19th and early 20th century, makes original use of stylisation, that characteristic device of the World of Art.

It is a bright, frosty day in his well-known picture *Shrovetide* (1916). Through the hoar-frosted branches you can see the roofs of houses with fluffy puffs of freezing smoke and a crowd of people in

← Nikolai Roerich

Visitors from Overseas. 1901
Oil on canvas. 85 × 112.5

Konstantin Bogayevsky

Sea Shore. 1907
Oil on canvas. 141 × 156

Boris Kustodiev

Shrovetide. 1916
Oil on canvas. 61 × 123

Zinaida Serebryakova   →

At the Dressing Table. Self-Portrait. 1909
Oil on canvas. 75 × 65

their Sunday best. In the transparent air you can almost hear the ring of bells, tambourines and children's laughter, the cries of street vendors and the cawing of startled crows. Like Yuon, Kustodiev makes use of a wide horizontal format. A future depicter of post-revolutionary public festivities, he introduces shop signs, painted horse harness and details of national dress into the picture. However, his real, everyday scenes are like the "popular woodcut pictures" (*lubok*) sold at bazaars and fairs. In the golden pink rays of the sun and the colourful, full-blooded forms a broad panorama of Russian winter unfolds, which serves the artist in different variants

as a background for many other works including his portrait of Chaliapin (1921).

The neo-classical trend of the 1900s and 1910s is perhaps reflected most clearly in the work of Zinaida Evgenievna Serebryakova (1884–1697). Incidentally she also tried her hand at monumental art and took part with other masters from the World of Art in painting the Kazan Station in Moscow under Alexander Benois in 1916–1918. Although her country house landscapes and interiors, like her figures too, whether they are peasants or members of her family, have an aura of domestic cosiness and privacy, the actual structure of her works reminds

one of classical easel and monumental works from the Italian Renaissance to Russian art of the late 18th and early 19th centuries.

A young woman's face with an open expression, not entirely void of mischief, gazes out from the mirror in Serebryakova's well-known self-portrait of 1909. The subtle palette, elegant contours of the objects on the dressing table (bottles, candlesticks and pins) and the graceful figure of the heroine are merely a device for the artist to express her ideal, which is natural simplicity.

At the turn of the century the Saratov painter Viktor Elpidiforovich Borisov-Musatov (1870–1905) became the bard of the disappearing "nests of the gentlefolk". In his famous painting *The Pond* (1902–1903 the figures of women in light, airy dresses form a single whole with the mirror-like surface of the pond, as they emerge from the quivering, "elusive" painterly texture of the canvas, an unsullied, dream-like medium. They are the artist's sister and fiancée, yet the "family" portrait lacks the fuss and sentimentality usually found in the genre. The main thing here is the fused tension of the rhythm, the "music" of enthralled contemplation. The bold dislocation of the spatial treatment of the composition (from a high, parabolic curve of the horizon outside our field of vision), the free interweaving of subdued pastel tones and the echoing of motifs, images and silhouettes produce a sense of time standing still, not so much real historical time, as an imaginary, personally experienced moment.

The synthetic experiments of Vrubel and Borisov-Musatov inspired the painters of the Blue Rose, a new artistic group set up in 1907 which included S.Yu. Sudeikin, N.N. Sapunov, P.S. Utkin, N.P. Ulyanov and, above all, P.V. Kuznetsov and M.S. Sariyan.

To express the inexpressible and penetrate beyond the limits of the visible world of objects, this symbolical creed of the Blue Rose became the active artistic programme of Nikolai Nikolayevich Sapunov (1880–1912). As if from a mysterious semi-slumber the curving outlines of precious porcelain vases emerge from the misty ultramarine depths of his large tempera still life *Vases, Flowers and Fruit* (1912). Immersed in the hazy background and surrounded by lush flowers and fruit, they strike powerful chords, variations on the theme of the unity of Beauty.

The porcelain figurines reminiscent of Hans Christian Anderson's shepherd and shepherdess in the composition *Still Life. Flowers and A Statuette* (1912) by Sergei Yurievich Sudeikin (1882–1946) radiate a childlike spontaneity. Yet behind the gallant naivety lurks a master of the generalised grotesque and behind the gentle brushstrokes the sharp eye of the decorative artist. Contained within the semi-oval canvas, which is like the wings of a stage, are two symmetrical vessels with white and pink cyclamen. The porcelain figurines are repeated in the painting behind them, in a complex interchange of "dead" and "alive", true and false, reality and its reflection in art. A painter of caféi interiors who died abroad, Sudeikin remained true all his life to the bizarre images of the baroque European theatre and the refined Chinese miniature, so dear to the masters of the Blue Rose.

Viktor Borisov-Musatov

The Pond. 1902–1903
Tempera on canvas. 177 × 216

← Nikolai Sapunov

Vases, Flowers and Fruit. 1912
Tempera on canvas. 147.2 × 115.8

Sergei Sudeikin

Flowers and a Statuette.
Late 1900s
Oil on canvas. 58 × 71

One of the achievements of the Blue Rose was to develop further the theme of the East beloved by the symbolists, which originated from direct impressions of life.

In the work of Pavel Varfolomeyevich Kuznetsov (1878–1968), whose youth was spent in the Trans-Volga steppes, this theme is developed in a series of paintings by the name of "Kirghiz Suite". In one of the pictures from this cycle, *Girl Asleep in a Tent* (1911) a girl, sheltered from the cares of the outside world by the "firmament" of an ancient Kirghiz yurt, is resting in the unchanging, comfortable world of her own sleep. The poetry of the everyday life of ordinary people, the age-old rhythm of its

simple rituals, are what leads the master to his broad plastic generalisations. This rhythm is also found in the painting *Mirage in the Steppe* (1912) where a "sign" hanging in the sky like a spectral hieroglyph draws into the inflorescence of oblique clouds the "world lines" of simple earthly motifs, such as grazing camels, the sleeping girl and the ghostly outlines of people.

The artist Martiros Sergeyevich Sariyan (1880–1972), who studied at the Moscow School of Painting, Sculpture and Architecture together with Kuznetsov (in Serov's studio, inter alia), remained faithful all his life in his canvases to the countryside of austere, mountainous Armenia. In an early work,

Pavel Kuznetsov

Girl Asleep in a Tent. 1911
Oil on canvas. 67 × 71.5

the small masterpiece *Street. Noon. Constantinople* (1910), painted during a journey to the East, a world of orange sun casts blue shadows on the flat surface of the canvas and fuses the sapphire depth of the sky with the sparse outlines of buildings that seem to be clambering upwards in the perspective of a small and remote oriental alley. Laconism is one of the most distinctive features of Sariyan's creative manner.

Unlike Sariyan, Nikolai Petrovich Krymov (1884–1958) deliberately focuses attention in his landscapes on details. In *A Windy Day* (1908) the smalled details of real life draw the spectator into a lively conventional world. To enhance the authenticity of his story the artist places in the foreground a barrel, a fence and a bridge over a ditch with dully gleaming water. Yet all these random, scattered objects, the small houses, the figures of restless animals, the people shielding their bodies against the wind, the cart on the receding road and, finally, the clouds of dust and dark thunderclouds, are full of the same whirlwind rhythm in anticipation of an imminent summer downpour. As if sensing future expressionistic experiments in painting, Krymov,

Martiros Sariyan

Street. Noon. Constantinople. 1910
Tempera on cardboard. 66 × 39

a master of the landscape and stage design, fills his almost toy-like, generalized woodcut (*lubok*) forms with sharp contrasts of light and shade and rich, deep emerald and bluish black tones.

The unity with nature that revealed itself to the masters of the Blue Rose in the forms of the lyrical painterly epic became a most important subject for the new generation of artists at this time. Its echoes can be seen in the provincial peasant and the "machine-like" urbanistic motifs of M.F. Larionov and N.S. Goncharova, K.S. Malevich and V.V. Kandinsky, V.E. Tatlin and M.Z. Chagall who make up another, very special page in the history of the Russian and, more broadly, world culture. Yet in spite of their break with the past, even the most radical manifestations of innovative, avant-garde thinking in Russia always retained a deep link with tradition, from mediaeval Russian art to the art of the late 19th and early 20th century. This heritage, particularly within the walls of the Tretyakov Gallery, still continues to inspire masters to new creative discoveries. With such a rich collection of art in its rooms, the familiar building in Lavrushinsky Pereulok remains to this day a unique focal point of Russian aesthetic consciousness.

Nikolai Krymov

A Windy Day. 1908
Oil on cardboard. 72 × 103.7

Natalia Goncharova

Peasants picking Apples. 1911
Oil on canvas. 104 × 97.5

Marc Chagall

Above the City. 1914–1918
Oil on canvas. 141 × 198

Semyon Shchedrin

Landscape with Ruins.
1799
Sepia, Indian ink,
brush and pen on paper
48 × 37

Drawing. 18th to the early 20th century

EVGENIA PLOTNIKOVA

The Tretyakov Gallery has a large and very fine collection of drawings. It is less accessible to members of the public than the paintings and is therefore not so well known. Due to the sensitivity of paper and the delicacy of the graphic media themselves these works cannot be displayed for long in the light (natural or artificial) and require special storage conditions. So drawings can only be on show in the gallery for a relatively brief period, but during this time they are invariably a source of great delight to visitors.

The collection was begun by the founder of the Gallery, Pavel Tretyakov. Although he gave preference to painting in his collecting, Tretyakov understood the role and importance of the drawing in artists' creative heritage. It was no accident that he acquired masses of drawings by his contemporaries and earlier masters. By the end of the 1880s he already possessed a considerable number of graphic works and intended to set up a special drawing department in the Gallery. At the time of his death, the collection consisted of 1619 drawings, watercolours and engravings. In the 1920s it was enriched by the addition of two large Moscow collections of drawings, those of I.E. Tsvetkov and I.S. Ostroukhov, which were formed at the same time as Tretyakov's.

The Tsvetkov collection was intended by its founder, I.E. Tsvetkov, to be a museum of drawings. Begun in the 1880s, it was remarkable for the breadth of the material and the number of Russian artists represented. As well as famous masters it included names that were almost unknown, yet have left their mark on the history of the Russian drawing. Tsvetkov's collection, which he presented to the city of Moscow in 1909, was in fact the first museum of Russian drawing. After nationalisation it became a branch of the Tretyakov Gallery, then, in 1925, an integral part of the present collection of drawings.

The I.S. Ostroukhov collection grew up at approximately the same time as the other two, and was acquired by the Gallery in 1929, after the death of the collector and the reorganisation of the museum that bore his name. As a collector Ilya Ostroukhov combined the erudition of a connoisseur of the history of art and the keen eye of a professional artist.

Brought together these three collections supplemented one another beautifully to form the nucleus of the Gallery's collection today. Throughout the 1920s it was actively expanded through the State Museum Fund. Since then this has been done through acquisitions. Of special value are the works (and there are many of them) presented as gifts, for which the Gallery is always deeply grateful.

The Gallery's collection represents the history of Russian drawings from the late 18th century.

Following the founding of the Academy of Arts (1757) the drawing was regarded as the basis of the three "finest arts" – painting, sculpture and architecture. This explains why we find classical examples of the drawing of this period in the work of such famous sculptors, architects, painters and engravers as Mikhail Kozlovsky, Vasily Bazhenov, Semyon Shchedrin and G.I. Skorodumov. Many of them were first-class draughtsmen. Two main genres dominate 18th-century drawing – the landscape and the portrait. The landscape drawing is represented in its most classical form in the work of the celebrated artist Semyon Fyodorovich Shchedrin (1745–1804). His *Landscape with Ruins* (1799) is executed in the traditions of the classical landscape with careful working of the foliage and the stone masonry of the ruins, which transforms these material objects into the beautiful, decorative fabric of a drawing.

The other genre that gained the right to independence at the end of the 18th century was the portrait drawing. A fine example is the *Profile Portrait of an Unknown Gentleman* (1788) by the superb draughtsman and sculptor Mikhail Ivanovich Kozlovsky (1753–1802). Executed in the then highly popular medium of sanguine, which lends the drawing special warmth, the profile portrait is in the form of a sculptural relief, and the gentle chiaroscuro modelling suggests light flowing over a marble surface. In this work one can sense the hand of a sculptor, his special vision of the world.

In the first half of the 19th century the art of drawing reached great professional heights. It became elevated to the same level as painting and sculpture, and in some respects even excelled them. It was at this time that drawings became items to be collected. They began to be regarded as having independent aesthetic value. The high level of general artistic culture and, in particular, the professional training of artists was the soil on which such brilliant masters of the drawing as Orest Kiprensky, Karl Bryullov and Alexander Ivanov grew up and reached the height of their talent.

A most striking and interesting feature of this period was the flowering of the pencil, and later watercolour, private portrait. The pencil portrait appeared at the same time as the flowering of lyrical poetry in Russian literature and the romance in Russian music. They are events of the same order. Their emergence and development were connected with a new trend in art – romanticism, with its intense interest in man's inner world of thoughts and feelings. The pencil portrait acquired special stylistic features in the work of Orest Adamovich Kiprensky (1782–1836), who is rightly regarded as the founder of this genre in Russian art. His portrait of Alexander Pavlovich Bakunin (1813), a school friend of A.S. Pushkin, belongs to his early period. It is executed in Italian pencil, which was popular at the time. The deep black strokes, which have a special velvety tone, are enlivened with pastel colour. The device of oblique shading round the outline of the figure is very characteristic of Kiprensky. The plane of the background, emphasised by diagonal lines and arranged artistically on the drawing, con-

Mikhail Kozlovsky

Profile Portrait of an Unknown Gentleman. 1788
Sanguine on paper. 49.6 × 34.5

Pyotr Sokolov

Portrait of Olga Golitsyna. 1847
Watercolour on cardboard. 33.1 × 26.1

Fyodor Tolstoy

*Red and White
Currants.* 1818
Gouache on brown
paper. 17, 4 × 23.8

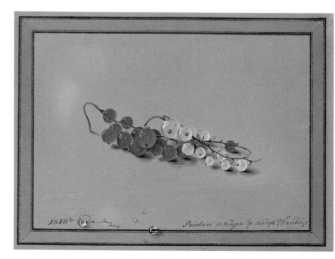

Karl Bryullov

Equestrian Portrait of Emilia and Evgeny Mussard. 1849
Watercolour heightened with white and Italian pencil on cardboard
69.3 × 51.2

Orest Kiprensky

Portrait of Alexander Bakunin. 1813
Italian pencil and pastel on paper. 30.2 × 25

firms the surface of the sheet in a frank reminder of
the conventions of graphic language. Kiprensky's
pencil portraits, produced in a period that witnessed
such events as the War of 1812 and the Decembrist
uprising, and was illumined by Pushkin's genius,
provide us with an invaluable poetic reminder of
this age. After Kiprensky many other graphic artists
of the day turned to the private portrait, making
their own individual contribution to its stylistics.

The distinctive art of the well-known sculptor,
medallist and draughtsman Fyodor Petrovich Tolstoy
(1783–1873) holds a special place in Russian artistic
culture. This master, who left a large graphic her-

itage, was a brilliant water-colourist. His famous
trompe-l'oeil watercolours of flowers and fruit painted to delight the eye lead one into a special micro-
world. Occasionally the artist plays tricks on the
spectator by adding a fly you want to swat or a
droplet you feel like brushing away.

His approach resembles that of a jeweller fash-
ioning a beautiful object and striving constantly for
the utmost precision and refinement of form. These
watercolours created by "Tolstoy's miraculous brush"
were extremely popular in his day and decorated the
pages of albums and the walls of drawing rooms.

Alongside the pencil portrait, the watercolour
portrait appeared in the first half of the 19th century
and became widespread. Its flowering is associated
with the name of Pyotr Fyodorovich Sokolov
(1791–1848), who devoted himself entirely to this
genre. Sokolov has a brilliant watercolour technique. His best portraits are executed with almost no
admixture of white. He achieves the utmost purity
and transparency of tone with an arsenal of artistic
devices that includes the paper itself, which shines
through the paint layer and enhances the resonance
of the colour. The small dimensions of the watercolour portrait and relative speed of painting it
made it widely accessible. Such portraits were commissioned for weddings and hung in studies or
drawing rooms. A small portrait could be taken on
a journey to remind you of someone dear. It was
portraits like these that the Decembrists took with
them into exile. Many artists were attracted by the
genre of the watercolour portrait. As a major artistic

Alexander Ivanov

The Annunciation
Late 1840s – 1850s
Watercolour heightened
with white and Italian
pencil on paper. 26 × 39

phenomenon, it was the product of its age and disappeared together it, recording for posterity the faces of people from those bygone days.

The work of Karl Pavlovich Bryullov (1799–1852) contains some fine specimens of the watercolour portrait. Unlike Sokolov's delicate sheets with their refined treatment of colour, Bryullov's portraits are full-blooded and substantial. You can sense the hand of the master painter in them. Bryullov created a new type of formal watercolour portrait treated as a compositional, often paired portrait against a landscape background.

A special place in the history of the Russian drawing belongs to Alexander Andreyevich Ivanov (1806–1858). His graphic heritage, later donated by his brother to the Moscow Public and Rumyantsev museums, was handed over to the Tretyakov Gallery in 1925 and is now the pride of

the collection. It is very extensive, consisting of studies from nature, preparatory drawings, genre and landscape watercolours and, finally, his famous Biblical sketches.

The cycle of Biblical sketches is a masterpiece of watercolour painting. Here Ivanov discovered some completely unexpected stylistic devices, previously unknown to his contemporaries. This large cycle (about 200 completed sheets and a large number of preparatory drawings), which consists of sketches for wall paintings, has the resonance of monumental frescoes. The majestic simplicity of the genre scenes alternates with the dramatic tension of the tragic scenes. Colour and light, the main devices of Ivanov's artistic language, open up hitherto unseen spatial depth on the small sheets, engendering a plastic expression of form and turning the white paper into a surface that radiates dazzling light. Depending

Pavel Fedotov

Promenading. 1837
Watercolour on paper. 26.5 × 21.4

The artist in a Life Guard Finland
Regiment uniform with his
father A.I. Fedotov and step-sister,
A.I. Kalashnikova

Vladimir Makovsky

A Lover of the Past. 1869
Watercolour on paper. 27.5 × 18.6

Ivan Kramskoy
Yuletide Fortune-Telling
Late 1870s – early 1880s
Italian pencil, sepia and shading
on paper. 25.8 × 34.5

on the emotional atmosphere of the scene the colour is either muted and restrained or full-blooded. The devices of watercolour painting are varied freely in accordance with the artist's aim. Each sheet has its own colouristic key. Sometimes the artist uses coloured paper (grey or brown), the tone of which unifies the polyphony of the splashes of colour. The expressive, flowing contours enhance the unusual plasticity of the composition. The emotional expression and profound philosophical meaning of these sketches ensure their everlasting relevance.

In the art of the mid-19th century the genre drawing came to the fore. Its development is associated with the name of Pavel Andreyevich Fedotov (1815–1852) in whose work the drawing held an

exceptional place. The artist had a perfect mastery of the pencil and worked in watercolour and sepia. His best-known series consists of sepia compositions on moral-critical themes, in which Fedotov proves to be a master of the vignette. His early watercolours executed in Moscow are not so well known to the public at large. They include one called *Promenading* (1837) which is both a genre scene and a kind of formal portrait of the young artist and his relatives, most touching in its naive sedateness. The life drawing and the sketch occupy an important place in Fedotov's graphic heritage. In these sheets the artist is searching for expressiveness in the language of line, that remarkable language which turns the ordinary and everyday into the aes-

Ivan Shishkin

"In the wild north…" 1891
Charcoal heightened with
white on paper. 56.4 × 43.2

Based on a poem by
M.Yu. Lermontov

Isaak Levitan

Autumn. 1890s
Watercolour and graphite
on paper. 31.5 × 44

thetically pleasing and artistic. The sketch drawing
as an independent work of art and an aesthetic cat-
egory was later to be developed, although in a new
capacity, in the work of those brilliant master
draughtsmen of the second half of the 19th century,
Ilya Repin and Valentin Serov.

The genre theme begun by Fedotov was continued by P.M. Shmelkov, P.P. Sokolov, V.E. Makovsky,
V.G. Perov and many Wanderer artists. In an age
when social problems were at the fore, however, it
was oil painting with its leading form, easel painting,
that held pride of place in representational art. For
most of the Wanderers the drawing, and particularly
the watercolour, lost their independent significance
and played a subsidiary role. The artists of this generation who paid most attention to the drawing and

watercolour were I.N. Kramskoy and N.A. Yaroshenko, and the landscapists A.K. Savrasov, F.A. Vasiliev, I.I. Shishkin and later V.D. Polenov and I.I. Levitan. The work of Isaak Ilyich Levitan (1860–1900)
includes few watercolours, yet they all show a subtle
feeling for nature. The artist understood the charm of
the watercolour. His sheet *Autumn* (1890s), painted
in barely perceptible, muted tones, creates an image of
dying nature full of poignant lyricism.

A new flowering of the graphic arts and the restor-
ing of their intrinsic artistic value to the drawing and
watercolour can be seen in the work of a remarkable
galaxy of masters – I.E. Repin, V.I. Surikov, V.A. Serov
and M.A. Vrubel.

The greatest draughtsman of the second half of
the 19th century, Ilya Yefimovich Repin (1844–1930),

Ilya Repin

At the Piano. 1905
Charcoal, Italian pencil, sanguine
and shading on paper. 45.5 × 29

who had perfect command of the various drawing techniques and drew often and fruitfully, left a colossal graphic heritage. His drawing manner changed over the decades, but he never lost his passionate love of the material world around him. Repin was a master of the three-dimensional, plastic, tonal drawing. His most characteristic pictorial manner is to combine the line or stroke with shading. His finest graphic portraits were produced in the 1880s. In his work the portrait sketch began to acquire independent value. In these rapid sketches Repin succeeded in poeticising and capturing the most characteristic features of his model and at the same time creating a legitimate artistic image. The artist reached the height of his talent as a draughtsman in the 1890s. His drawing became extremely free and picturesque. In such graphic works as the portraits of E. Duse (1891) and V.A. Serov (1901) executed in charcoal on canvas, the artist produced images of monumental stature. In the early 1890s Repin's drawings grew lighter and brighter. He was attracted by impressionist experiments. His models became immersed in light and air and the lines began to vibrate. Light shading gave the drawing a special transparency. The artist often enlivened a black drawing with sanguine. One such sheet is *At the Piano* (1905), in which strokes that barely touch the paper and fine shading produce a texture full of light and air.

The great flowering of the drawing is associated with the name of Vasily Ivanovich Surikov (1848–

Vasily Surikov
Seville. 1910
Watercolour on paper. 35 × 25

1916), a born master of colour with a keen sense of the colouristic richness of the world. It is no accident that the watercolour dominates his graphic heritage. The artist saw his future canvases primarily in terms of colour, planning the main combinations in watercolour sketches. He worked in watercolour all his life, but there are two periods when he reached his height in this medium. The first was in the 1880s, when he went to Italy. The images of Italy created by Surikov in his beloved cold bluish-grey gamma, full of diffused light and damp air, show a superb sense of colour harmony. The second is associated with his visit to Spain in 1910. In the sheets of the Spanish series the full elemental force of colour seems to burst through. These vibrant, intense colours are assembled into a single orchestra that resounds with a wild ecstasy. Accurately conveyed colour combinations transform the white sheet into a dazzling surface. Transparent paint is applied to damp paper in broad, free washes with no attempt to conceal the conventionality of the device. The colour, which speaks out boldly in Surikov, is extremely emotional. It is either jubilantly festive or dramatically expressive. In their artistic stylistics Surikov's later watercolours belong to the twentieth century.

Two brilliant names are associated with the art of drawing at the turn of the century. They are Valentin Serov and Mikhail Vrubel.

Valentin Alexandrovich Serov (1865–1911) never parted with the pencil throughout his creative life. Drawing was his natural element. His colossal graphic heritage includes a wide range of genres. There are rapid sketches and academic studies, landscapes and the history genre, antique themes and nude studies, caricatures and animal drawings. But most productive of all for Serov were his beloved portrait drawings. A pupil of Ilya Repin and Pavel Chistyakov, he firmly mastered their system of drawing from life, strong formal structure and interest in the Old Masters. His early drawings show detailed, careful modelling. Later, in his search for a

generalised and clear graphic language, Serov arrived at the laconic, linear drawing. In the drawings of his classical period (1890s–1900s) his mastery of plastic form is such that he can render the subtlest curves and movements by superbly expressive lines. This period saw the birth of a special type of Serov drawing, capable of saying a great deal with a minimum of devices. What is outwardly left unsaid actually speaks volumes. For each portrait image Serov finds a special graphic language that reveals the character of the sitter clearly. Thus, a few melodious, smooth lines create the poetic image of the ballerina Tamara Karsavina (1885– 1911); the features of actors and actresses from the Moscow Art Theatre are summed up in short, rapid strokes; the powerful image of Fyodor Chaliapin (1905) is created with strong, confident lines, affirming the remarkable force and breadth of the great singer; and in the sketch for his portrait of the dancer Ida Rubinshtein (1905) the decorative outline of the figure is conveyed with grotesque caricature in a broken, angular contour. Serov also worked a great deal in watercolour. For his sensitive taste the special charm of this difficult medium lay in the refined restraint of the colour and beautiful matt surface.

Mikhail Alexandrovich Vrubel (1856–1910) was an unexcelled draughtsman, whose work shows rare imagination, perfect taste and a strongly individual style characteristic of him alone. In his treatment of form one can sense the Chistyakov school, although transformed by his own talent. The rhythm of faceted planes full of tense, agitated strokes creates

Valentin Serov

*Portrait of the ballerina
Tamara Karsavina.* 1909
Graphite on paper. 42.8 × 26.7

Mikhail Vrubel

Italy. Neapolitan Night
Sketch for stage curtain. 1891
Watercolour, graphite
and whiting on paper mounted
on cardboard. 57.5 × 70

Mikhail Vrubel

Venice. Bridge of Sighs
1892–1893
Watercolour on gold-edged
cardboard. 25.7 × 12.6

Mikhail Vrubel

A Rose. 1904
Watercolour and graphite on paper
mounted on cardboard. 29.8 × 18.5

the vibrating surfaces of his pencil drawings. Only Vrubel knew how to bring the texture of a drawing alive like that, to fill it with a quivering sense of man's inner state. He was also a water-colourist of the highest quality. For him the watercolour was the testing stone on which he tried out ways of mastering plastic colour. Vrubel's watercolours are a whole world of tiny jewels, a glittering mosaic of coloured stones. More than anyone else, the artist understood the true qualities of the watercolour, its luminescence, transparency, and rich reflexes that create the shimmering surface of the sheet. His heightened perception enabled him to understand the full tonal richness and polychrome of the world. With equal care he examines the human face and the texture of cloth, the intricate forms of a flower and the depths of the background. Through the power of his own imagination he gives the most prosaic objects a sense of mystery and hidden life. In Vrubel's work the 19th-century watercolour reached its height. The artist and art historian Igor Grabar rightly called him "the finest water-colourist in the whole history of Russian art".

The work of Viktor Elpidiforovich Borisov-Musatov (1870–1905) stands out among the masters of the late 19th and early 20th century for its remarkable originality. He was one of the few artists of the period who preserved the watercolour medium in all its purity and mastered it with professional brilliance. An artist of great refinement and subtlety, he created poetic watercolour compositions and portraits full of musical rhythm. His large

Viktor Borisov-Musatov

Lady in Blue. 1902
Watercolour and pastel
on paper mounted
on canvas. 81.5 × 62.5

Konstantin Somov

*The Echo of Time
Past.* 1903
Watercolour and gouache
on paper mounted on
cardboard. 61 × 64

Evgeny Lanceray →

*Empress Elizabeth at
Tsarskoye Selo.* 1905
Gouache on paper
43.5 × 62

watercolours executed in faded tones like old tapestries lead the spectator into a dreamlike world of phantom images. Borosov-Musatov's work is stylistically close and akin in spirit to that of the World of Art.

The emergence onto the artistic stage of the talented constellation of artists from this creative association marked a new period in the history of Russian graphic art. In spite of differences in their creative personalities A.N. Benois, K.A. Somov, M.V. Dobuzhinsky, L.S. Bakst, B.M. Kustodiev, E.E.Lanceray and others were united by a common striving for high professional skill and the search for a modern language in art. The heritage of the World

of Art members impresses one with its great thematic diversity and range of creative experiments. On the one hand, there was a turning to the art of the past, to history and popular life, and on the other, the constant desire to work in all spheres where the artist's eye was needed (the theatre, book publishing and monumental decorative painting).

In their search for new expressive devices artists arrived at mixed media, something hitherto unknown. The wet techniques of watercolour, gouache and tempera were combined with dry ones, such as pencil, charcoal and pastel. A new kind of graphic art appeared on paper or cardboard, which was later to complicate the task of restoration. The

← Konstantin Somov

*Portrait of the Poet
Alexander Blok.* 1907
Graphite, coloured pencil and
gouache on paper. 38.2 × 30

Lev Bakst

Salome. Costume sketch. 1908
Graphite, gouache, whiting,
Indian ink, gold and silver on
paper. 46.9 × 30.3

work of each member of the World of Art is great and diverse. The most classical master in terms of professional command of drawing media and materials was Konstantin Andreyevich Somov (1869–1939). His graphic works include some splendid pencil portraits of great refinement and poetic watercolour landscapes with a fine feeling for barely perceptible states of nature, which are executed in free brushstrokes with interwoven splashes of colour. A special Somov theme is his imaginative treatment of the past, which enables him to travel back to bygone days with their customs, refined manners and dress, introducing notes of theatricality and sadness into the treatment of the images. In Somov's work the art of the miniature was reborn.

His small watercolours, although stylistically connected with the twentieth century, retain the devices of miniature painting, the loving care of the old art. The retrospective theme was also taken up by other masters.

The image of old St Petersburg runs like a leit-motif through the work of Alexander Nikolayevich Benois (1870–1960) and Yevgeny Yevgenievich Lanceray (1875–1946), who portrayed the town of the Petrine age with a remarkable feeling for the period. Alexander Benois was the leader and inspirer of the World of Art association, an erudite art historian and subtle artist with a refined sense of colour harmony. His series of sheets on Versailles, the artist's favourite theme, are full of classical serenity

Mstislav Dobuzhinsky

Man in Glasses. Portrait of the poet Konstantin Sunnerberg. 1905–1906
Charcoal and watercolour heightened with white on paper mounted on cardboard. 63.3 × 99.5

Boris Kustodiev

A Fair. 1906
Gouache on paper mounted on cardboard. 66.5 × 88.5

and solemnity. Executed in a dignified, restrained colour range, they preserve graphic precision in the drawing and composition. The artist rarely works in pure watercolour. He likes a matt, velvety surface, and therefore makes active use of white, preferring dense gouache and even tempera. Most of the World of Art members were skilled at bringing the past to life. It is not surprising that many of them worked with great success in the theatre.

Mstislav Valerianovich Dobuzhinsky (1875–1957) was a brilliant artist with a special graphic vision. His favourite theme was the modern city viewed through the contrast of past and present, the city in its tragic aspect, joyless and monotonous, staring out through the eye sockets of its windows.

The drab colour introduced into the strictly graphic texture of the drawing evokes a mood of sadness. In his splendid portrait of the poet Konstantin Alexandrovich Sunnerberg (Constantin Erberg) entitled *Man in Glasses* (1905–1906), the theme of the hostility of the city provides the emotional key to the treatment of the artistic image. The man has turned his back on the soulless townscape that is engulfing him and radiates a sense of hopelessness and isolation. The portrait symbolises, as it were, the creative world outlook of the artist at the beginning of the twentieth century. By contrast the theme of vivid national character in the work of such masters as B.M. Kustodiev, F.A. Malyavin and A.P. Ryabushkin, who were fascinated by popular festiv-

Kuzma Petrov-Vodkin

Head of a Girl. 1912
Watercolour and pressed charcoal
on paper. 33.8 × 24.2

Boris Grigoriev

Two Female Figures. 1902
Graphite on paper. 34.7 × 21.2

ities, decorative national dress and the specific charm of the Russian character strikes a joyous note.

The next generation of artists, who appeared in the 1910s amid presentiments of revolutionary upheavals and world cataclysms, was a generation of rebels who overthrew artistic traditions. Many talented masters of this period belonging to different artistic trends were excellent draughtsmen. The drawing was for them an active way of expressing their own personality. In these pre-revolutionary years graphic art became a kind of laboratory for experimenting. A strong interest in primitivist art and the popular woodcut (*lubok*) can be found in the work of Mikhail Fyodorovich Larionov (1881–1964) and Natalia Goncharova (1881–1962). By deliberately simplifying and coarsening nature, Larionov achieves a high degree of expressiveness. Goncharova possessed remarkable decorative talent in drawing. Her splendid "Spanish Women" (circa 1916) (in memory of a visit to that country) demonstrates her brilliant mastery as a draughtsman. Spread over the paper, as it were, the drawing turns the whole sheet into an intricate graphic pattern.

Alexander Yevgenievich Yakovlev (1887–1938) and Vasily Ivanovich Shukhayev (1887–1973), neo-classicist artists who turned to academic traditions, attached prime importance to the drawing. The constraint of their plastic form gives their work a look of cold, rational mastery, however.

Boris Dmitrievich Grigoriev (1886–1939), an artist with an individual, highly temperamental manner of drawing, was an outstanding draughts-man of this generation. He has points of contact with neo-classicism, but his drawing shows an enviable diversity and virtuosity. Usually executed in lead pencil, Grigoriev's sheets impress by the unexpected grotesqueness of the images and at the same time the refinement of their artistic language. The sharp plasticity of his drawing is the result of extremely laconic, flexible lines combined with light, three-dimensional shading. They always retain the measure of illusory volume and decorative flatness so important in a graphic work.

The graphic heritage of Kuzma Sergeyevich Petrov-Vodkin (1878–1939) demonstrates the high professional skill of a draughtsman with an analytical cast of mind. His drawings of the pre-revolutionary period are marked by a search for the "grand style" in art. The rare talent of a monumentalist gives his sheets a special significance. Stylistically they show plastic clarity and refinement of form as well as a sculptural monolithic quality. The *Head of a Girl* (1912), executed as a preparatory study for the painting *Mother* (1913) acquires independent aesthetic value. The austere beauty of the Russian Madonna, full of inner dignity and spiritual purity, attains a classical epic unity.

Together with Petrov-Vodkin mention must be made of his younger contemporaries, a whole galaxy of talented draughtsmen such as N.I. Altman, Yu.P. Annenkov, P.V. Miturich, L.A. Bruni, V.V. Lebedev and N.A. Tyrsa who developed and emerged in this period, continuing the fine traditions of the Russian drawing in the new age.

← Natalia Goncharova

Spanish Women. Circa 1916
Graphite on paper. 64.2 × 49

Alexander Yakovlev

Dancing Girl. Early 1920s
Sanguine on paper. 133.6 × 90.2

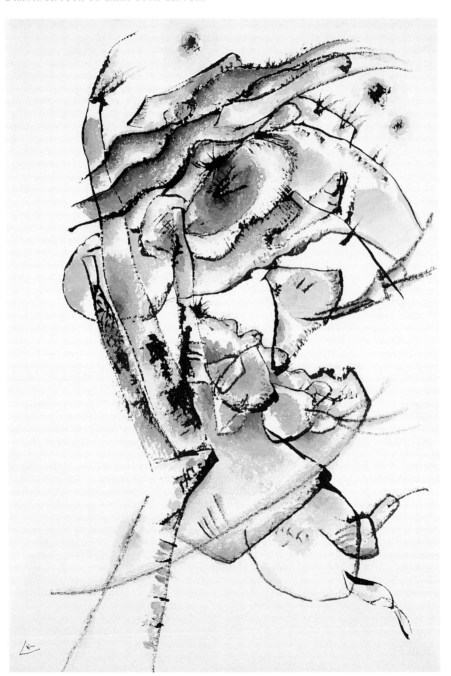

Vasily Kandinsky

Abstract Composition
1915–1917
Watercolour. Indian ink and
brush on paper. 30.9 × 21

Pavel Filonov

Self-portrait. 1909–1910
Pen, brush, brown and black ink
on paper. 6.6 × 8.1

The works of avant-garde artists born in Russia who brought fame to their native land in the twentieth century resound like a magnificent, echoing chord. Various trends of the avant-garde are reflected in the unique graphics of Kandinsky, Malevich, Popova, Pougny and Chagall, which demonstrate the artists' perception of the world on the threshold of the new century.

The history of Russian drawing is, of course, far broader and more diverse than it has been possible to show in this brief outline. Here we have indicated only the main stages and trends, the most significant phenomena and the most celebrated names that form landmarks in its development. The Gallery's selection of drawings displayed in its rooms will greatly add to and enrich the visitor's impressions.

Illustrated guide

MASTERPIECES
OF THE STATE
TRETYAKOV GALLERY

Russian Art from the 12th
to early 20th century

PAINTING • DRAWING

Second edition

Формат 60 × 90/8
Бумага мелованная
Гарнитура Garamond
Печать офсетная
Печ. л. 20,0
Тираж 5 000 экз.

Отпечатано в Финляндии

Издательство «Красная площадь»
127422, Москва, Дмитровский пр., 8/1
RUSSIA